The ITSM Iron Triangle

Incidents, changes and problems

Stories in transforming ITIL® best practice into operational success

DANIEL McLEAN

IT Governance Publishing

Every possible effort has been made to ensure that the information contained in this book is accurate at the time of going to press, and the publisher and the author cannot accept responsibility for any errors or omissions, however caused. Any opinions expressed in this book are those of the author, not the publisher. Websites identified are for reference only, not endorsement, and any website visits are always at the reader's own risk. No responsibility for loss or damage occasioned to any person acting, or refraining from action, as a result of the material in this publication can be accepted by the publisher or the author.

ITIL® is a registered trade mark of the Cabinet Office. The Swirl logo™ is a trade mark of the Cabinet Office.
© Crown copyright 2011. Cabinet Office.

Apart from any fair dealing for the purposes of research or private study, or criticism or review, as permitted under the Copyright, Designs and Patents Act 1988, this publication may only be reproduced, stored or transmitted, in any form, or by any means, with the prior permission in writing of the publisher or, in the case of reprographic reproduction, in accordance with the terms of licences issued by the Copyright Licensing Agency. Enquiries concerning reproduction outside those terms should be sent to the publisher at the following address:

IT Governance Publishing
IT Governance Limited
Unit 3, Clive Court
Bartholomew's Walk
Cambridgeshire Business Park
Ely
Cambridgeshire
CB7 4EH
United Kingdom

www.itgovernance.co.uk

© D McLean 2012

The author has asserted the rights of the author under the Copyright, Designs and Patents Act, 1988, to be identified as the author of this work.

First published in the United Kingdom in 2012
by IT Governance Publishing.

ISBN 978-1-84928-317-5

The ITSM Iron Triangle

Incidents, changes and problems

Stories in transforming ITIL® best practice
into operational success

PREFACE

People often struggle implementing process based on best practice standards. Rarely is this due to a failure to understand the standards, the tools, or the technology. Usually, it is a failure to appreciate, and deal with, issues surrounding changing people's behaviors.

Implementing process is all about changing behavior. The words in the phrase, ***People – Process – Tools***, are in that order for a reason. If people don't embrace the activity, then the Process and Tools won't matter. Changing people's behavior is one of the hardest things we do in business, and what IT people often find most difficult.

IT has a little secret no one likes to talk about. High performers understand that IT is more dependent on conversations between people, and the behaviors of people, for its success, than on the state of its technology. It's as true in IT as it is in any other part of the company.

Unfortunately, IT has a terrible history when dealing with people issues involving dialogue and changes in behaviors. These elements are mentioned in some standards, but with little specific guidance or examples.

This is one in a series of books designed to help you do more than just survive these issues. These books will show you how others dealt with the same situations you face every day. These books look at what worked, what failed and traps to avoid.

Learn from their lessons and avoid their mistakes.

ABOUT THE AUTHOR

Mr McLean is a consultant who has designed, implemented and operated processes supporting ITSM for over 10 years. He has worked in IT for over 20 years. He was a peer reviewer during development of the OGC ITIL®[1] v3 Service Strategy standard. He has developed and delivered ITIL courseware customized to company-specific operational practices and needs. He has worked in the US and the Middle East.

Mr McLean's consultancy focuses on fusing best practices from multiple ITSM relevant standards, into practical operational processes optimized for each organization's particular environment and needs. He provides this support at the design, implementation and daily operation levels.

Among other honours, Mr McLean holds an ITIL Manager's Certificate in IT Service Management, an ISO20000 Consultant Manager Certificate, and an ISO20000 Professional: Management and Improvement of ITSM Processes Certificate.

Mr McLean holds both Bachelor's and Master's degrees from Cornell University.

Mr McLean resides in Chicago, Illinois, US.

---

[1] ITIL® is a registered trade mark of the Cabinet Office.

ACKNOWLEDGEMENTS

I wish to thank the following people, without whom none of this would have been possible.

My clients, users and customers, for allowing me to learn and improve by serving them.

My managers and leaders, for trusting me with opportunities that made me grow.

My peers, for challenging my habits and making me continually assess and improve my deliverables.

We would like to thank Chris Evans – ITSM Specialist and ir H.L. (Maarten) Souw RE IT-Auditor, UWV, for their most helpful contributions in reviewing the manuscript.

My teachers and mentors, for their tolerance of my ignorance, persistence in their instruction, and patience with my endless questions.

My employees, students and mentees, for allowing me to grow by helping them learn.

My family, for tolerating my single-minded focus.

And my wife, Patricia, for being my rock and constant companion.

CONTENTS

Introduction 1
Chapter 1: Change in Assignment 3
Chapter 2: Into the Fire 13
Chapter 3: Turning up the Heat 23
Chapter 4: Searching for the Right Place to Start 33
Chapter 5: Investigating the Wetware 49
Chapter 6: Managing Service Outages 69
Chapter 7: Time to Refocus 79
Chapter 8: The Five Questions 91
Chapter 9: What is that Light at the End of
    the Tunnel? 103
Chapter 10: Not Everyone likes Answers 113
Chapter 11: Why Service Outages are like
    Dandelions 123
Chapter 12: When No One is Around 133
Chapter 13: The Right Thing the Wrong Way 143
Chapter 14: Going Through them Changes 155
Chapter 15: Some Fingers Point and Some
    Hands Clap 169
Chapter 16: What Have you Done for me Today? 177
ITG Resources 183

INTRODUCTION

Incident, problem and change management are interrelated processes which are foundational to IT success. High-performing IT organizations design, implement and execute them well.

Successful implementation of these processes requires being able to change people's behaviors as effectively as you change technology. That's where IT people struggle, and it's an area with little specific, or practical, coverage in the best practice standards.

Overcoming these issues is more critical to successfully implementing IT processes than memorizing process life cycle steps.

This narrative story provides a collection of lessons from real-world experiences in changing people's behavior, whilst building these foundational processes.

You may already have met some of the characters in the book. How about leaders whose support vacillates based on the situation? Ever had peers who only support you if it stymies their rivals? What about people who are deceptive and distort critical data, based on goals unrelated to yours?

Please remember that this story has been fictionalized. All persons, places, organizations and events appearing in this work are fictitious. Any resemblance to real people, living or dead, is entirely coincidental. Any resemblance to actual places, organizations or events is entirely coincidental.

CHAPTER 1: CHANGE IN ASSIGNMENT

Each new job was always different. No two companies, or bosses, were ever exactly the same. The good news was that after three months onboard, I was still excited about this one, and wanted to keep it. The job market was terrible, and it had taken me a long time to find something. No way I wanted to go back into that job-hunting swamp anytime soon.

Today I was a little worried. Ramesh, my boss, had just called. He told me to drop everything and immediately meet him in the CIO's office. Even during the brief phone call, I could hear loud argumentative voices in the background, and that couldn't be good.

I hadn't been here long enough to merit special praise for anything. I was really worried about why they wanted to meet with me. All the way over, I kept working through the lists of things I'd been asked to do, promised to deliver, or actually completed. I checked each for any flaw that might put me in jeopardy of losing my job.

The CIO's door was closed, and I could hear the voice of Jessica, our CIO, right through the door. I couldn't make out the words, but it was pretty clear she wasn't handing out congratulations. I took a deep breath, and rapped on the door. Ramesh yelled, "Come in," before I had finished the second knock.

Jessica hung up the phone as I entered, and stomped over to the window, whacking the credenza with her pen as she passed. Ramesh pointed to the empty chair beside him and I

1: Change in Assignment

sat down. Still staring out the window, Jessica started talking.

"That was the CEO and COO on the phone. They'd just left a meeting with the VP of sales, who apparently convinced them that any shortfall in revenue this quarter was due to the failure of IT to keep our systems up and running. Each month we promise them that the number of outages will go down, and every month for the last six months, outages have gone up. Yesterday's disruption was the final straw. That outage took an entire region offline for two hours, during the busiest part of the day. The most embarrassing part was that it was virtually identical to what happened last month, and the month before. Remember them? The ones we said were now fixed and wouldn't happen again."

Jessica turned around slowly, her face flushed. She walked silently over to her desk and sat down opposite us. She began nervously tapping her pen against the top of her desk.

I started to relax. Outages were something Sarah managed. She was the incident manager. We both worked for Ramesh, but incidents were outside my scope, and I was happy with that. I liked to be able to sleep through the entire night. I had helped Sarah with outages in the past, and would keep doing so. It struck me as strange that Sarah wasn't here and I was. After all, Jessica was talking about Sarah's area of accountability.

Ramesh turned to me and said, "We need to make fixing these continual outages a priority."

"Shouldn't Sarah be part of this discussion? I'll help her if I can, but shouldn't she have a voice in designing the solution?" I asked.

1: Change in Assignment

Jessica cut me off. "As of 9 am this morning, Sarah is no longer affiliated with our company. She has been given the freedom to create even greater successes elsewhere. We all wish her luck in her new endeavors, and are sure she will do an outstanding job in wherever her new role takes her. There will be an announcement going out this afternoon. But until then, please keep this confidential to the people in this room."

So Sarah got fired for all the outages? It sounded like they shot the messenger, rather than deal with the message. Worse, it seemed to be their response of choice. Right after I'd started working here; Sarah had told me about replacing the previous owner of incident management, after they were given the "opportunity to be more successful elsewhere." I was starting to have an uneasy feeling about this meeting.

Jessica got up, walked around her desk, and sat down beside me. She leaned over, put a hand on my shoulder, and smiled. In a quiet, but firm voice, she said "Outages have to stop. Not in a year. Not in six months. We need it solved now. They are limiting the success of the company. And without company success, there won't be enough funding to support IT. And none of us wants to deal with what would happen if I no longer had the funds to support the people, and the programs, currently in place."

"Are you talking about potentially laying people off?" I asked.

"I'm an officer of the company," she said. "I can't, and won't, use words like that lightly. Let's just leave it at none of us wants to go there. That's why you're here. Ramesh and I have gone through your background, and we think you are the one who will make this a success."

1: Change in Assignment

Jessica laughed quietly. "Besides, it is time we got some return on the investment we made by paying for you to take that ITIL Foundation Course last month, right?" Her face got serious and she sat paused for a moment. "So what do you say? Can we count on you? Are you up to being a hero in everyone's eyes and knowing you are preventing something bad from happening?"

I tried not to wince. Sarah had been doing the job for a while, and had a lot more training and experience than I did. She'd worked for the company almost nine years. I tried to assume best intent, but the more I thought about it, the more it felt like my boss, and the CIO, had colluded to put me between them and an ugly situation. That way, if things didn't improve, they would have someone else to blame. At my old job, we used to call those people, "Disposables."

Ramesh forced an unnatural smile and chimed in, "And you already know that expenses are being cut back across the board, just to meet the current expense levels. So we can't fund any consultants for this, and everyone else is pretty much allocated out on critical projects. You'll have to be an influencer and negotiator if you need any more hands to fix this. But I'm sure you are more than capable of fixing the outage situation by yourself. All you have to do is drive down the number of service outages. Should be simple for someone as smart as you. But if you need my support for anything, just let me know. I am 100% with you."

"That goes for me, too," smiled Jessica. "You have my full support for this. If you need some capital money for tools, I can probably find a few dollars somewhere," she smiled. "VPs have a few tricks up their sleeves. No promises, but

1: Change in Assignment

maybe we can even justify a promotion for you after this is all fixed. You'd like that, wouldn't you?"

"And don't worry about your current work," added Ramesh. "I'm assigning Tracey to take over your old role. She's earned a promotion, and based on my conversation with her, she is very excited to be taking over your current role, and picking up some additional responsibility. I want these outages to have your undivided attention." Ramesh paused for a moment. "That is, if you are willing to step up and show Jessica, and the rest of the company, what a great decision it was to hire you. The decision is totally up to you."

So this wasn't a consultation as to whether or not I wanted to take this on. It was a directed task. I tried to scramble and buy some extra time to make this work.

"I'm very grateful, and a little overwhelmed, that after only a couple of months you are giving me such a great and visible opportunity. But maybe the reason we've had trouble fixing it before, is that we haven't had enough hands on it. Isn't there any way I could bring in some experts from the outside? Maybe they would have some out of the box solutions to jump start our efforts. Even a few dollars would help."

Jessica stood up and walked back around to her side of the desk. With both hands on her desk, she leaned across it towards me and said, "There really isn't the time to select a firm, bring them in, and get them up to speed, even if we had the money to do it. Besides, you're the expert here. There is no one in the organization better suited to this situation than you. What could some outsider tell you that you don't already know?"

1: Change in Assignment

She gestured to a table in the corner of her office, piled high with books and media. "Sarah always bought me a copy of every manual, standard and book she ordered. I'm not sure why. She assured me that everything we needed was in there." Jessica waved her pen at the pile. "I always used to tell her that if I knew all that stuff, she'd be out of a job, and that she was lucky it's just too academic and conceptual for my little brain," she laughed. "I need action and results, not theory. I haven't gotten around to reading them, but I know you can master them quickly. I'm sure the answer to any of your questions will be in there somewhere."

Jessica called out to her administrative assistant. "Sue, will you please get us a cart, so we can get these books out of here, and free up some space in my office? Our new superhero is going to use them to solve our outage problems. Just put them on a cart for Chris, please."

"Congratulations on volunteering to solve the outage problem for us," said Ramesh. "You've validated my decision in hiring you."

"Our expectations are that you'll have a time line of actions and deliverables for us by the end of the week, and that we'll see some positive trends starting in the next 30 days. The business can't wait much longer, and you know how demanding they can be," added Jessica.

Ramesh smiled, "Of course, you could always decide to overachieve and make things happen sooner. I promise we won't complain."

I winced, and wondered if I should dust off my last resume and start looking now. It had only been a couple of months. Maybe my contacts would still be active. But the job

1: Change in Assignment

market was so bad right now. At least if I start looking now, I will be 30 days ahead when they throw me under the bus in a month.

Feeling a little like a condemned prisoner, I forced a weak smile and said, "Unless you have anything else, I guess I'd better get started."

"That's what I like to hear," said Ramesh. "Make us proud. And don't forget. We expect a readout of your plan and time line in a week. And if you need anything in the interim, just come hunt me down. I'm there for you."

I stood up and headed for the door. Both Ramesh and Jessica were silent as I walked. I was grateful they were going to support me so completely. I would probably need them to command some people to comply with process changes, if I had any hope of making this work. A small part of me was still afraid I was just a disposable buffer to help them keep their jobs. But that was probably a normal fear. Once the first crisis developed and they stepped up, I knew I'd feel better.

Just before I reached the doorway, Jessica broke the silence in a light sing-songy voice. Her tone reminded me of the voice adults use when talking to infants. "Oh, and will you please close the door on your way out, and ask my admin to get Sully, the CEO, on the phone."

As soon as the door closed behind me, Ramesh and Jessica began a conversation, but it wasn't loud enough for me to understand a word of it.

I headed straight for Sarah's old cube. Once inside, I could still feel her upbeat perky vibe. That was something I wished I had right now. I sat down in her chair and stared at her family photos arranged around the desk. Little moments

1: Change in Assignment

of bliss standing as counterpoint to the trauma she'd just endured. I hoped she was doing okay. Getting fired is always traumatic. Getting fired for failing at an impossible task, is even more so. All of those smiling faces brought the reality of my situation back to me. Security must have walked her straight to the door with no allowance to clean out her personnel effects. This was serious business. There were significantly unpleasant consequences for me if I didn't make things better. I only wish I knew how. The ITIL Foundation training had been great, but it all seemed so theoretical and abstract at this point. There was so much to do. I didn't know how to turn that classroom work into something real. Where should I start? It was overwhelming.

I hadn't been there more than a few minutes, when Sean stuck his head in.

"Sarah, I love the way you've fixed your hair. But your new wardrobe definitely needs a make-over," he laughed. "I'm looking for Sarah. I want to go over some of the details of the outage from yesterday. Have you seen her?"

I shook my head. Sean had spent his entire working life at this company. He'd been around almost since the beginning, and his fingers had been in almost everything IT had ever built or installed. I'd met him the first week I came onboard, and he always seemed to know the answer to any question I could ask. I liked working with him because he knew so much about the way this organization operated, and about all those things people never write down.

I was about to ask Sean for some advice on what to do next, when both our phones lit up with texts. Sean immediately said, "Mierda, we just had another Severity One outage. Looks like the entire Northeast region just dropped off the network. I gotta go. We gotta find Sarah so she can manage

1: Change in Assignment

the event. If she's not here, I don't know who will coordinate the communications, and make sure everyone is there."

I stood up. "Looks like that's me."

"Very funny," said Sean. "But we don't have time for jokes right now. The business is down and we've got to get it restored. We need Sarah."

I shook my head. "You won't find her here anymore."

Sean stopped and gave me a look like only someone who has seen it all could. "Oh, so it's like that is it? I'll have to call her later and see how she is doing." With a deep sigh, he said, "Well, let's go. Time for your initiation by fire."

As I followed Sean out of the cube, my phone rang again. It was Jessica, the CIO.

1: Change in Assignment

Tips that would have helped Chris

Leadership direction to begin an ITSM initiative will most likely be a tactical response on their part, in reaction to recent specific issues, rather than a strategic plan to implement a full series of ITIL life cycle processes. Don't feel you need to develop and implement a complete ITSM strategic plan to begin. Try to drive forward tactically, by narrowly focusing on the most appropriate process to resolve their issue. Your success there can later be the launching point for a broader, integrated, ITSM effort.

It is common to take over this type of tactical challenge from an incumbent who is either no longer with the company, or unwilling to help transition you. Make every effort with what is available, to understand what they have done to solve the problem. At a minimum, you will learn what did not work, or work fast enough. Trying to obtain that feedback from leadership is generally not worth the effort, as they will be focused on the solution state, and not on the detailed design information you need.

CHAPTER 2: INTO THE FIRE

They call them War Rooms for a reason. Ours was a commandeered windowless conference room. An old wrinkled sheet of copy paper with the phrase "RESERVED FOR WAR ROOM," was taped askew to the door. The word "WAR" circled by an ancient coffee stain. Inside were a long rectangular table, and an enormous whiteboard on the wall at the far end. The room was overfilled with people, and everyone seemed to be talking at once. On the table, two speakerphones were hosting different conversations while people clustered around them. Those not clustered around the phones were sitting around the table, or against the wall, in chairs wheeled in from nearby offices for the occasion. Judging by the stains on the carpet, and the marks on the wall, the room hadn't been cleaned in a long time.

Sean nudged me and whispered, "This is the part where the incident manager takes charge of the meeting." He did an exaggerated look around the room and said, "Since I don't see Sarah here, I guess that means you."

This was my first War Room at the company. I knew Sean was right, and I needed to take charge now that Sarah was gone. I hesitated, because I wasn't sure I could start the meeting, or control it, without guidance from someone like Sean who was more familiar with the people and workings of the company.

Sean's phone rang and he stepped just outside the room to take the call. It didn't seem like he realized I could hear his end of the conversation, as well as see him.

2: Into the Fire

"Yes, Jessica," said Sean. "Chris is here now. I made sure of that. Running the meeting is another story." He paused and nodded.

Sean kept talking and gesturing, "Yes, I can imagine sales is pretty torqued about now. Can you hold them off for a little while, until I get things organized and we can give you an estimate?"

Sean nodded several times while listening. "Okay. I understand." After a pause, he turned his back to me and whispered quietly, but I could still make out his words, "I'm worried Chris can't handle this – not the right type for incident management. You sure you don't want me to take over and get it under control?" After a few nods he said, "Okay," and hung up.

I tried motioning to people to quiet down and sit, but almost no one paid any attention. I started asking people one by one, when Sean said to me, "Watch and learn."

Sean slammed the whiteboard hard with the flat of his hand. Before the sound faded, he yelled, "Shut up and sit down. Now!"

The room quickly got silent, except for the clatter of keyboards, and the beeping of messages leaving and arriving on a variety of electronic devices.

Sean whispered to me, "Good thing I'm your friend. I had to go to bat for you with Jessica just now. She was ready to punt you out and have me take over. But I convinced her you needed some time to succeed." He paused, "So you can owe me one for that. It's your show, but you better get to it. Patience is not an inexhaustible resource."

2: Into the Fire

Before I could respond, my phone beeped as a series of text messages came rolling in. The first one was a hysterical all-caps message from Jason, the VP of sales and marketing, wanting to know when they could begin making sales again. The next one was from Jessica, the CIO. That one was less hysterical, but wanting a firm commitment when it would be fixed. And then one from Ramesh followed, asking for a detailed status on the cause and time to fix.

I decided to chance waiting until I knew more.

Mimicking Sean, I slammed my hand flat on the table and told the room, "Settle down. We need to get to work. I need an update on what we know about what happened to take the business off the network. Who's got some updates?"

Nicola, leader of the firewall team, was chugging a can of energy drink and had two more on the table in front of him. I remembered that he'd been putting in a number of approved changes last night, so he probably hadn't been to sleep yet. In his thick Ukrainian-accented English he said, "Where is Sarah and who are you?"

In the chaos of the moment, I started to say something, but remembered that Jessica and Ramesh had told me not to say anything about Sarah until there was a formal announcement that put the proper perspective on her, "transition". Their instructions had probably been the right thing to say because of the way they seemed to identify incident response with Sarah. I was having enough trouble trying to figure out how to keep this group focused. Her rapid departure would probably have been a major distraction from getting the service restored.

Fortunately, Ramesh's voice rose up on one of the speakerphone conversations. "This is Ramesh. I can answer

2: Into the Fire

that. Sarah is handling something else for Jessica right now. Chris will be leading restoration from ... "

Nicola didn't let him finish. "Why are we changing? What is the reason? Does Chris know how do to Sarah's job? I have never seen Chris here before. Do you realize this risks further impacting the business, if Chris cannot perform at Sarah's level? This is a distraction that we do not need."

Irritation coated Ramesh's voice. "Nicola, Jessica has made this decision. We all have to have faith in her as our leader, and that she has made the right decision for the company as a whole. I know that she is counting on you, and the rest of the IT staff, to rely on Chris' leadership to get this outage resolved, so we can better support our business partners. She expects each of you to give Chris your complete co-operation and support, so we can minimize the impact on the business of this service disruption. If you disagree with Jessica, I will be happy to arrange some one-on-one time between her and you later today. Any questions?"

Nicola tossed his empty energy drink can at the trash can, but missed. "Understood," he snapped. "That won't be necessary."

That was my cue. I stepped up to the head of the table. "My name is Chris and I'll be leading the restoration of this disruption. What are the ... "

Sean jumped over my words and began to write on the whiteboard. "Okay, let's help Chris. You all know the drill. What do we know? Where did the alert come from? Who is impacted? How severe is it? Is anybody currently working on it?"

At first I was ticked at Sean for stealing my role, but as I watched him work, I was amazed at how, within a few

2: Into the Fire

minutes, Sean pulled and effectively organized on the whiteboard all the information the group had about the incident, added his own substantial knowledge, and assigned owners to restoration tasks.

"Good, so we are all agreed then?" said Sean as he filled in the last bit of information on the whiteboard. "The root cause was the print server crashing."

Nicola stood up and began drawing lines on the whiteboard that looked like a cross between an organization chart and a sentence diagram.

"What's that?" I asked.

Nicola stopped and stared at me like I had asked him why he was breathing. "Obviously you have no training in root cause." He waved his hand at the board. This is an Ishikawa fishbone diagram, to determine root cause. We need to know how to prevent it from happening again."

I shook my head, "We shouldn't focus on the root cause right now. We know what broke and took the store printing offline. We need to make sure we can get that service working for the business again. That is job one. We can worry about cause later."

"You must understand, Chris," said Nicola. "The root cause is what we seek. By identifying it, we learn about what fails in our environment. That is the primary function of our incident team; to respond to weaknesses, then identify how to prevent them from happening again. Otherwise we risk fixing the wrong thing."

Nicola turned back to the whiteboard and continued talking as he worked. "To ensure maximum efficiency, we have instituted a standard root cause methodology. Every

2: Into the Fire

incident has its root cause done the same way, using the same methodology. That ensures we use tools with which we are experienced, so we know we will have the correct cause for the incident, before we waste efforts on repairing the wrong thing."

Nicola began filling out the fishbone and highlighting the conditions involved in the outage in red. When I asked if all of those items connected to the outage were really contributors to the outage, Nicola shook his head. "You see. You do not understand the proper way to conduct incident root cause. You will learn the importance of these things if you pay attention to how we work."

In a few minutes, Nicola had finished filling out the chart and came to the same conclusion as Sean. The only difference was that Sean understood it instinctively, whereas Nicola was totally dependent on the methodology.

"Clearly, it is the Windows® platform team that owns this root cause. Glad I'm not getting tagged for that outage," said Nicola. "I'm already on the 'Grid' too many times."

Before I could ask what the "Grid" was, Sean pointed to a worn page from a flipchart someone had taped onto the whiteboard. It was covered with handwritten squares, with people's names across the top, and dates down the side. Some of the intersecting squares had numbers. Some were blank. A few of the names had lines through them, crossing them out. "It's a rolling matrix by team and date, of the number of outages they own," said Sean.

I pointed to the crossed out names.

"If you get too many, you get set free to extend your success elsewhere." A few people in the room laughed. "This isn't the official one. Only leadership gets to see that.

2: Into the Fire

This is our copy we keep, so that you can see when you're getting in trouble."

"How many marks do you have to have to be ... set free?" I asked.

Sean shook his head. "Don't know. No one has been able to figure out the algorithm leadership uses. You never really know how many mistakes are tolerated, and how many are too much. It seems to vary, depending on which VP is looking at it, and how loud the business is yelling." He crossed out Sarah's name and stepped back, like a painter checking his perspective. "Something less than what Sarah had, that's for sure."

I watched on my laptop as the rebooted Windows® print servers came back up. As soon as they seemed stable, I tested them out, to make sure they worked. I thought that would be a nice little piece of proactive work for my first day.

Satisfied they were running again, I stepped into the hall, and returned the call from Jason, the VP of sales and marketing. I was 10 minutes later than I had promised in my text, but figured he wouldn't mind, now that everything was working again.

"Hi, this is Chris from IT. I'm just following up to let you know that ... "

"To let me know that everything IT touches turns to crap. Where the hell have you been?" he screamed into the phone. "I don't appreciate being dragged away every few hours just to tell IT how to do its job. Every night I get called because IT is incompetent and can't keep their servers running, but it now appears that either none of you own watches' or else you don't believe in meeting your

2: Into the Fire

commitments. Which is it? Are you clueless or just plain irresponsible?"

I took two slow breaths and fought the impulse to respond immediately. As the urge passed, I responded, "I'm very sorry the service went down. I wish I could go back and prevent it from happening, but I cannot. What I can do, is promise you we will take steps to prevent it from happening again. I will be personally responsible for that to you."

Jason interrupted me, "That's what your predecessor said and look where it got her. But I'm going to hold you to your commitment," he paused for a moment to let his words sink in. "And after you fail, I'll hold your successor accountable, too. And if that doesn't work, I'll see to it that IT gets outsourced to a firm that knows what it's doing."

He paused for a moment, and then said something to someone else in the room with him. All I caught was, " ... be right there."

Jason was a little more composed when he said, "You do understand that if I don't meet my commitments, then IT doesn't get money for its fancy toys, don't you? And if you can't meet even the most basic of tasks, and learn not to break anything, then perhaps we are giving IT too much money, and you're all distracted by your techie toys. Think about how IT would do if we cut your funding by 20%, or if we started outsourcing your work. Consider that, the next time you get the urge to break something."

He hung up without even saying goodbye. Actually, I was grateful. Besides, we'd gotten the service back up and running. It hadn't been pretty, but at least it got done. I could hardly wait to tell Ramesh all the details. I knew he

2: Into the Fire

was going to be happy and very pleased with my performance.

> **Tips that would have helped Chris**
>
> Your users rarely understand when their IT services are disrupted, regardless of the cause. These events impact their ability to meet their goals, earn their compensation, and retain their jobs. They feel injured. Allow them to vent their feelings to you without being defensive. Despite the words they use, it is about the situation and not about you. Once they have said their piece, then you can start to work together on a factual basis.
>
> Implementing ITSM processes requires you to lead through influence. If you try to mimic the style of other leaders, it will come off as unauthentic. Borrow elements from different leaders, but always make it your own.
>
> Similar to the way people are sized-up during the first 30 seconds of a job interview, so are leaders new to a situation immediately sized-up by the participants. If you are in charge, take charge. You should set the example by being confident, decisive, transparent and accountable.

CHAPTER 3: TURNING UP THE HEAT

I stepped out of the War Room just as Ramesh came down the hall. He immediately pulled me aside. We stood three steps away from the door as people filed out.

I was grinning when I said, "So what did you think of my performance running my first incident?"

"I listened to the whole thing and I want you to know that was the worst example of leadership I have ever seen in my life," he snapped back. "If Sean hadn't been there, it would have been chaos. Nothing would have gotten done. I'm just glad I wasn't in the meeting room, so I didn't have to watch your performance, as well as listen to it. If you can't get a better handle on these meetings, no one will follow your leadership and nothing will get done. Remember, you volunteered to reduce the number of incidents. No one forced you to take this job. You took it to get a quick promotion."

People leaving the meeting slowed down, like gawkers at a car accident. There is some slightly perverse desire in some people that makes them eager to hear, or see a disaster, as long as it doesn't directly involve them.

I tried hard not to let my frustration show at this public pillorying. I didn't so much mind the criticism, as I did having it conducted in front of the people I'm supposed to lead through influence. I put on my best supplicant voice and said, "Ramesh, I'd really like to get the rest of your feedback. Should we step into the conference room and continue this discussion one-on-one, to make sure I get the full benefit of your feedback?"

3: Turning up the Heat

"No, I don't have time. I've got to go meet with Jason, on behalf of Jessica, and try to repair the damage you've done to the business. He told her all about your arrogant, flippant, disrespectful attitude. Furthermore, there is nothing I have to say to you about this that can't be heard by everyone. I'm just reinforcing what they have all seen. And if they didn't see it, then they don't belong here either."

At that last comment, the cluster of people lingering nearby dispersed quickly. It was one thing to watch someone else get reprimanded, but if the blame spread, no one wanted to be around.

Either Ramesh, Jessica or Jason was lying about my discussion with Jason. I had no idea why, and it really made no difference. There was no way I could successfully argue with Ramesh about my conversation with Jason.

"Ramesh, be reasonable," I said. "You just gave me this assignment today. We fixed this incident and got everything working. But realistically, it will take some time to figure out why this happened, and how it is connected to the other incidents."

"It's not about being reasonable, Chris. It's all about meeting the needs of the business. Even Sarah was about to produce a root cause by the time the service was restored. Sean could do it. Nicola could do it. Even a 10 year old child could do it. That is our job. If we're not up to it, then it's time to change people."

"But you weren't even at the meeting," I blurted. "You just phoned in. You couldn't have seen everything that went on, or what the dynamics were?" I wondered if he had seen, or knew, that the employees had their own version of the

3: Turning up the Heat

leadership incident grid. But did leadership really have one, or was it just an attempt, by employees, to make sense of leadership's actions?

"Makes no difference," said Ramesh. "What specifically did you do? Did you identify the fault? Did you develop the solution?"

"Well, no. I was focused on ensuring the team worked together to get the business ... "

Ramesh cut me off before I could finish. "Your answer is no, you did nothing. Instead, you totally sidestepped a great opportunity to show some leadership, and figure out why these are happening. You had all the right people there in the room, and rather than leading them toward preventing these incidents, you got in their way. Not only did you not make it better, you actually made it worse. What's wrong with you? Don't you have the guts to lead?"

"I am a good leader. And I'm doing my job as a leader, by telling you that we need some additional time to reduce the number of incidents. We may have restored this one, but it was exactly like the one yesterday, and the one the week before. It will probably happen again."

"It better not. That's why you are here," said Ramesh, more sternly this time. "You heard Jessica. Fix it, so we will stop having these outages."

He was being unreasonable. I needed to make him understand that there was nothing in the meeting that was going to help us stop service disruptions.

Before I could speak, his phone rang. With a wave of his hand, he cut me off and walked away, chatting with his caller. He stopped, turned, and in a loud voice said, "Chris,

3: Turning up the Heat

you have a meeting with Jessica and Jason, in Jessica's office, at 1 pm. I suggest you have some answers by then."

Without waiting for my response, he resumed his phone call, and continued away; walking and talking at the same time. I was glad to see him go. I was surprised Sarah hadn't quit before they fired her.

I got back to my cubicle, so I could confirm the service was still up, and the incident was over. But I never got a chance. Sean was there just as I sat down. He leaned over the wall and grinned in a way that made me feel very uncomfortable, like I was prey.

"You know what you did wrong back there?" he said. "You missed a big chance to nail the reason we keep having these outages. Do you have any idea how hard it is to get all those SMEs together in a single room, unless it is a crisis? That's why we do root cause in the incident war room. But don't worry; I'm sure we'll have another one just like this one by the end of the week."

He chuckled and added, "If you're worried about Ramesh firing you, rest easy. I just talked with him on the phone. He wanted my input on the meeting and my opinion of you. Fortunately, I was able to convince him that even though you just had 15 people spend two hours on the outage, and cost the company 4,000 dollars in time alone, without a single step towards preventing these outages, he needed to give you more time to get things right. It was the same message I gave to Jessica before the meeting when she called."

He leaned closer and quietly said, "But if I were you, I'd spend more time at the next one worrying about how to get

3: Turning up the Heat

those servers back up faster. If you don't, you'll never figure out how to prevent the incidents."

"It was more important to get the service back up first," I snapped. "You saw the rat-holes people wanted to go down, analyzing the cause rather than how to get it working. If I'd let them run free, they'd have spent days arguing who was at fault for the outage."

Sean walked around and into my cube. He sat down on the opposite side of the desk. "Relax, Chris. Don't forget, I'm your friend here. Right now, I may be the only one you have. I only have your best interests at heart. I'm just trying to give you the benefit of my experience. But if you don't want my help, I can shut up and let you wander around on your own."

"Sorry," I mumbled. "I just don't appreciate getting my guts ripped out in public ... especially in front of that audience."

"Don't worry," said Sean. "It's happens to all of us. Everyone understands it is just part of the motivation strategy here. It's nothing personal. It's just business. You'll do fine. I'll see to that."

I still hadn't figured Sean out yet. There were moments when he seemed to be waiting for just the right moment to toss me under the bus, and others when he seemed like a genuine friend who wanted to help me succeed.

It wasn't until Luther, one of the Windows® system administrators, sent me a text and asked if everything was working okay with the server that I realized I had almost forgotten about the incident. As I sent him back a thank you, Sean got up and started to leave.

3: Turning up the Heat

Sean was nearly out when I stopped him, "I spoke to Jason, but who should I contact on the business to see if they are happy with things now?"

He laughed and said, "Well, your phone hasn't gone off, so that means it must be doing okay. You may have noticed we don't have any fancy monitoring software in our environments. We have something better than a sophisticated monitoring tool. We have thousands of users who scream at the drop of a hat. So don't worry. They'll let you know if you are not doing a good job."

He took two steps and then added, "Besides, it would take you a long time to figure out who to call. You could always try Basil. He used to work in IT, before moving over to the business. He was involved in setting up the network in the first place many years ago. I think he's moved on to something else over in marketing, but maybe he can point you in the right direction."

"You mean we don't know?" I started scanning the trouble ticket, looking for the person who called it in.

"If you're looking for the ticket originator," said Sean, "Save yourself some effort. That field doesn't work in the ticketing system, so no one ever bothers to fill it out, and when users call they usually don't take their names because they don't want them to feel inhibited about calling problems in. Who knows, one of the creaky old probes in our 10-year-old monitoring tool might have sent in the alert. I doubt it, but you never know. But that's not important. If no one is calling you or the data centre, then everything must be working. Let it go and move on. There will be others to worry about."

3: Turning up the Heat

Sean leaned forward and smiled. "And once people figure out you're Sarah's replacement, you'll have so much work, you won't have time to look up that kind of stuff."

I shook my head. This was a mess. No wonder Sarah got fired. Or was there another reason?

"Sean," I asked. "Do you know why Sarah was pushed out?"

Sean furtively looked around; almost as if he were making sure no one was listening. In a quiet voice he said, "You're new here, and so you probably don't fully understand the culture yet. I'll give you a piece of advice. If you want to stay employed here, you'll learn not to talk about, or even mention, people who leadership has given the, 'freedom to achieve even more success elsewhere.' Those people become non-entities, as if they never existed. The only good part is that for the first month after they are gone, you can blame them for anything that is wrong; from things they worked on, to why there are never enough towels in the bathroom."

"Okay, so what did she do wrong?"

"She volunteered to solve the trouble with all these incidents, and when she hadn't fixed it after an interval of time that leadership felt should have been enough, they made her a non-person. And now that she's gone, blame her for everything that doesn't work. You'll be on the hot seat with leadership breathing down your neck soon enough."

"But I didn't volunteer for this ... not really."

Sean smiled and started to walk away. "Neither did she. No one ever really volunteers for things like this."

3: Turning up the Heat

I headed to Jessica's office early. I did not want to be late. I'd called Basil and gotten a voicemail that he was out for another two weeks on vacation. When I called his back-up number, the person covering for him knew nothing about the incident. In fact, they seemed surprised he was out on vacation.

I started to wonder if they did any real work in marketing, and that if I could only get a job there, then my life would be real easy.

Then I realized that was probably exactly how people in marketing felt about IT.

3: Turning up the Heat

Tips that would have helped Chris

When you start, or take over the development of a solution, many people will want to offer you advice on the right way to work. Try to think of that input as data points. When deciding how to work, consider all of that advice, but make sure what you do is your own.

Don't be surprised if people appear inconsistent between their actions and their words. Try to learn as quickly as possible which people are authentic and remain the same in both public and private. Those are people you can rely on, even if they disagree with you.

People who have been working on similar, but incomplete projects, for extended periods of time, may be cynical and negative about the possibilities for success. Don't take on their attitudes of acceptance and powerlessness. Your confidence and belief in your abilities is one of the greatest strengths you have.

CHAPTER 4: SEARCHING FOR THE RIGHT PLACE TO START

My meeting with Jessica, Ramesh and Jason had been a ritualized and highly structured beat-down, organized by organizational stature and the degree of suffering you felt you had endured.

Jason yelled at Jessica. She then yelled at Ramesh. Ramesh yelled at me, and since there was no one else in the room that was lower in the organization, I just had to sit there and take it.

Jason didn't want to hear about plans, or efforts, or goals. All he wanted was an ironclad guarantee that it would never happen again. Fortunately, Jessica was smart enough not to give it to him. He didn't take it very well. I didn't know if it was just Jason personally, or customer facing people in general, that make them seem so demanding and unreasonable when they get to be the customer. I guess they treat IT the way they often get treated.

As I left the meeting, I tried to put it all behind me. But I knew I wouldn't survive much longer if I didn't find a solution to reducing the outages. What we were doing wasn't working, and no one here seemed to have any idea of anything different to do. I hoped all those ITIL and ITSM books Jessica gave me would have some answers. But right now it was the end of the day on Friday and I was going out with my friends for a few hours. I'd do a better job of figuring out a solution if I gave myself a little time off.

4: Searching for the Right Place to Start

After I finished a long Friday night with my friends, I locked myself away and spent the rest of the weekend slogging through the books Jessica had given me. Some of it I remembered from my ITIL course, but these were a lot more detailed. I hoped that was a good sign.

I was determined to find the answer I needed on how to stop our incidents. I'd fallen asleep several times working my way through the minutia in the ITIL standards, gotten lost trying to figure out the limited notes and documentation from our ticketing system, and by Sunday, had even built a footrest with documents I'd waded through, each purporting to have the solution to our situation.

And they all had the solution ... but only up to a point. And that was my dilemma.

They were all impressive pieces of work. Like all great ideas, the basic concepts seemed simple and obvious once you understood them. Each had strengths and added to my knowledge.

I was fascinated by the way the incident, problem and change processes leveraged each other to the benefit of our users; much like a fire department protects the local residents.

Those in incident management were the fire-fighters, the first responders. They were the ones tasked with stopping further damage and putting the fire out. The problem management team were like the arson squad, picking through the ashes to understand why the fire broke out and what could be done to prevent it from recurring here, or elsewhere in the neighbourhood. While those in change management were like the building inspectors, the gatekeepers working hard to ensure that based on what the

4: Searching for the Right Place to Start

arson squad learned, nothing was put into the neighbourhood that might threaten anyone's safety and security in the future. Each made perfect sense to me and I understood something that had never reached me in my brief class. Having any one of them would yield benefits, but if I could get all three working, they would leverage each other, giving us more than the sum of their parts.

I was also really impressed with how much ITIL turned the old-school IT perspective upside down; shifting IT's focus from inside-out to outside-in. Inside-out was IT creating what it thought were the best tools available, and offering them to the users. But outside-in was ITIL turning that perspective around, to understanding what was important to the users, and providing them with solutions to meet those needs. It was elegant, efficient and effective.

But knowledge isn't the same as a solution. Knowledge is what you get from going to school. Solutions are what you get from real-world experience. Sometimes the distance from knowledge to solutions is an apparently uncrossable chasm.

Knowing what was in the books, and having the experience to adapt them to my current situation, were very different things. Knowledge was generalized and fleeting, unless you used it. Experience was earned and yours forever.

Even if I had all this knowledge inside me, I really didn't have the experience to make it relevant to my situation. And the scary part was that right now, I was probably the most knowledgeable person on ITIL and ITSM in the entire company.

4: Searching for the Right Place to Start

The one comforting thought I had, was that the only way one gains experience is by doing. And that in the real world, doing is often a very messy activity.

By Sunday night, swarms of process charts, life cycles and roles spun through my head, but I still couldn't unlock the key that would tell me how to match the theory to reality. I'd looked everywhere, and couldn't find it in any of the books. Worse, I couldn't even find a place to start. Beginnings are important, and I wanted to make the right choice the first time.

I read and re-read the material over and over. I started to doubt my ability. I just knew the tactics and procedures had to be in the books somewhere. I needed something practical, manageable and executable.

I didn't want this to be my life's work. I didn't want to be an expert consultant, or advance the theory of the next version of ITIL. Smarter people than I could have that, as far as I was concerned. The later it got, the more I just wanted to get Ramesh off my back and keep my job.

By early Sunday evening I began to suspect I was having a hard time seeing the solution, because I was trying to absorb too much information. My mind was burnt. I needed to change the air in my head. I grabbed my keys and went out to get something to eat. Perhaps the change of scenery would reset my thoughts.

I wasn't looking for a fine dining experience, just planning to tank-up on regular. There were plenty of places that fitted the bill nearby; all franchised theme eateries, with modified bar food that were nearly indistinguishable from each other. Eventually I picked one, because I didn't have

4: Searching for the Right Place to Start

to turn left to enter the parking lot, and it had a traffic light, so I could easily get out and back to work.

The restaurant was crowded and noisy. It was half-price pitchers of draft night, and that meant at least 30 minutes before I could get a table. As I stood wondering whether it made sense to go somewhere else, I spotted Jahred, an old friend of mine from college.

This was a casual restaurant, and he was heavily overdressed in what was clearly a very expensive, custom suit. He looked more appropriate giving a pitch to the Board of Directors than slurping down an order of fried wing poppets, slathered in fiery hot sauce, while sucking down generic beer that had been brewed to be inoffensive, rather than good. I waved and managed to get his attention. It had been more than a couple of years, but he recognized me and waved me over.

Jahred stood and shook my hand. "Chris, how have you been? You look great!"

I smiled, "You look fantastic, although perhaps a little overdressed for this place. Or are you interviewing for a position as a maître d'?"

"If I were the maître d', then you'd ask me for a better table, and I'd have to ask you for a 20 dollar tip."

He laughed. "Seriously, I'm on the road and the airline lost my luggage again, so I'm wearing work clothes. But I had them send my suitcase on to my next city, so I'll pick it up when I land tomorrow morning. It'll probably be there before I am."

4: Searching for the Right Place to Start

"You travel for work?" I asked, slightly embarrassed that I hadn't kept up enough to even know what he did for a living.

"Better to ask when am I not travelling. But that's part of being a consultant. You can't very well manage clients long distance. You need to look them in the eye and press the flesh if you're going to have credibility. People need to establish a personal connection with you if you are going to succeed. And no matter what you do, it's all about people."

I nodded and thought maybe he ought to work in IT for a while and try to live without technology, or even processes like ITIL.

"I see how that helps build good relations with your clients, but what about the rest of your life? Doesn't that make it hard to have strong relationships with your family and friends? I mean, if you're always gone, that must strain things a lot. Surely some of the long-term clients are adults and don't need all that face time, do they?"

Jahred took a loud slurp of beer and shook his head. "You gotta do whatever it takes to make your clients happy. If it wasn't for them, there'd be no reason for you to be around. Besides, when I'm on the road, the company picks up all my expenses; meals, cleaning, entertainment ... everything."

He leaned across the table. I could tell by the smell of his breath that this might not be his first pitcher of beer. "And it's always easy to round those expenses up a little, with a little creative accounting, if you know what I mean," he whispered. "It's like free money. I'll bet you don't get that kind of perk at your job."

4: Searching for the Right Place to Start

He tossed a sauce covered hunk of something fried into his mouth, talking as he chewed. "As far as family life, it has to come second. Sure, there's a high divorce rate in consulting. That's why you either stay single and get your fun on the road, or find a spouse who understands that it's not forever. At the rate I'm billing, in a couple of years I can leave consulting and my wife can open that bed and breakfast on Nantucket Island she always wanted, while we are still both young enough to enjoy it. You gotta do the work before you get the cookie."

Jahred pulled a business card from his pocket and handed it to me with two hands, such that I could read the text even before I took it. Even with all the beer in him, it was so fluidly done, I figured he must have practised it for hours.

"If you think you want to try life's fast lane, just let me know, and I'll put in a good word for you at the firm."

"And what are you doing?" he asked.

I felt naked without any business cards, or other proof of my work, as if somehow that made me less valuable.

"Just got a new job. Been there less than three months and they've switched me to a new assignment."

"I knew you were a player," smiled Jahred, as he tried to high-five me. I missed his cue and he quickly pulled his hand back to the fried bits covered in sauce. "You must be doing something right."

"Maybe. I'm taking over a high-visibility project from someone they just fired for not producing the results they want. No one in the company understands how to make it successful, or has been able to do it. I'm supposed to become the expert and make their problems go away fast …

4: Searching for the Right Place to Start

or else I get fired, too. The visibility is great, but I'm a little nervous about the risk of getting tossed under the bus like my predecessor."

Jahred shook his head, "Chris, you're looking at this all wrong. You've been given an incredible gift. This is a career-making opportunity. It's the type of thing the consultants in our firm do every day. This is life in the big leagues. You can turn every event into an opportunity. That's what winners do." He raised his sauce-covered thumb and forefinger in the shape of the letter "L" against his forehead. "Or you can be a loser and cast yourself as the perpetual victim."

If Jahred was being honest and not drunk, maybe I could pull some ideas out of him to help me. "Have you ever done IT process consulting? Do you know about incident management? I need some specific tactics and steps I can take to reduce the number of incidents."

"No way. But I don't need to. That's for losers and junior wonks new to the firm. I'm strictly a big picture strategy and transformational guy. My success is based on managing the two most important pieces of the client relationship; the vision and the client. The rest is just execution. Anyone can do that."

Jahred poured the last of the beer from the pitcher into his glass and took a big swallow. "You can't see the truth of this because you've let the company leadership push you too far down in the execution detail. You've lost sight of the vision. Remember the old joke about a consultant being someone you hire to look at your watch and tell you what time it is?"

I nodded slowly, but still didn't see the connection.

4: Searching for the Right Place to Start

"In my work, I always find that the answers are all there. If I simply work with the client, they end up telling me what they want and what they think the solution should be. Once I have that, I just repackage it, add some special sauce to fill in the gaps, and I've got everything I need to close the deal. With the deal signed, I just turn it over to their staff for execution, and move on to my next opportunity. The one thing my clients really want is reassurance that what they are doing is right. All the best practices do that for you. You just need to explain those best practices to company leadership, and relate it to their situation. Once you do that, call it done, stick a fork in it, and move on."

Jahred was starting to slur his words a little. Judging by his condition, he'd either been hitting drinking hard, or been here a long time. I'm not sure I cared. I just wanted to hear more if it could help me solve my situation.

"But how do I make those celestial perfect-world truisms real and operational? I understand the standards backwards and forwards," I lied. "But if I don't do something practical that produces results, I'll lose my job, too."

"Do more by doing less," he mumbled, and slurped some more beer. "It's the secret sauce that makes it work. Keep it simple for your clients. Their world is complicated enough as it is."

He put his glass down, leaned across the table, and pointed a finger at me. "I really shouldn't share this secret with you. Since we're both O.G. I'll share it with you," he said quietly, as if he were revealing a state secret.

"I used to think like you do, too," he said. "I know you'd never believe that looking at me now, but it's true. I was once as wonky as you, if you can believe that. Then one of

4: Searching for the Right Place to Start

the senior partners ... my mentor in the firm to be specific, straightened me out. He became my mentor after I'd covered for him one day when his wife called, and he was not where he was supposed to be ... if you get my meaning. From then on out, we had a great relationship. He helped me by having my back for relationships in the firm and I helped him by having his back for his relationships ... outside the firm." Jahred winked and smiled.

"You can't be the expert in everything for everyone," he said. "It's like the C-level executives I deal with all the time. They don't know the specifics about anything. They just know where they want to be, and how soon they want to be there. That's the vision thing. They set up the vision and the timetable. Then it's up to their staff to figure out the mundane bits. No one can know it all. That's unrealistic, and more importantly, it's not what they get paid for."

I tried to imagine presenting what I found out to Jessica and having her issue orders for her staff to make it happen. The picture seemed hard to believe, but maybe there was a kernel of truth in Jahred's ramblings. He was very experienced and very successful. Maybe the problem was that I was making this too complicated.

"And when it comes to the next layer down," said Jahred. "Because you know the C-levels are going to want you to share your knowledge with their staff ... just explain the principles to them in a way they can understand, and step aside, so they can do what they do best ... marshal their teams and instruct them to go execute. If you explain it right, the benefits of doing it will be obvious to them. Once they understand what the vision is and why it's important, they'll step right up and ensure their teams make it work at

4: Searching for the Right Place to Start

the detailed level. Give them the credit for their capability that they deserve."

"You make it sound easy," I mumbled.

"Look, Chris," Jahred leaned across the table and poked his sauce stained finger at me; this time barely two inches from my nose. His beer breath almost overpowering. "There are two kinds of people in the business world ... those who lead and those who execute. Are you a leader, or some loser who just executes orders?"

"I'm a leader, of course," I responded immediately, as I'd been conditioned to, without even thinking. But as the words left my mouth, I had some doubts. Jahred seemed to have all the answers, and here I was wandering around in the wilderness trying to figure out how to even start. Could I be that much off the path?

"Then act like one. Sell your clients on the importance ... "

"These aren't clients," I interrupted. "These are the senior leaders in my company ... people way above me in the chain of command."

"Same thing. Client, customer, user, partner, business ... whatever. They are your targets and you're trying to close them on the deal. You're the leader for this and they want to be led. Do you believe in what you're selling them? If they do what you ask, will it make their organization better?"

I thought about the synergy between incident, problem and change management, for starters. "Well yes, of course."

"Then it's up to you to present the ideas in a simple way they can understand and embrace. Sell them on the benefits of doing what you want. These are C-level executives. If

4: Searching for the Right Place to Start

they believe in the vision, they won't worry about the mundane details. You don't need to do the work for them; you just need to show them the goal. Do that and they'll be overwhelmed with the truth and rightness in what you're proposing. Do it right, and before you even get done, they'll be so excited they'll already be figuring out who they want to handle the implementation and execution details. Then all you have to do is get their signature on the deal and collect the check. "

"Jahred, like I said, they are not externals. You're talking about people inside the company; my senior co-workers. I don't get paid extra for getting them to like my ideas."

He shook his head and smiled. "There you go thinking small again. You still get paid, just not money. You get more promotions, better opportunities, bigger raises, stock options ... the whole thing. Look, Chris; either go big, or go home. Otherwise, you'll be one of those little people all your life."

Jahred stood up and swayed, as he sucked the last of the beer foam from his glass. He was more than a little drunk. "I gotta go get some rest. I'm flying out at the crack of dawn and I need to make some calls before I go to sleep. It was great to see you again. I hope I was able to help clear the fog."

He took three steps towards the exit then stopped, turned, and wagged his finger at me one last time. "And remember; explain it to them so they can understand the vision. If they can't understand your message, then you're giving them too much detail. Once they get your message, you just sit back and let them handle the execution. That's all there is to it. Just don't get wrapped up in the mundane details, or you'll lose them."

4: Searching for the Right Place to Start

And with that, he disappeared into the crowd and was gone.

By the time I got home it was nearly 1 am. I kept wondering if Jahred was really right. He made it sound so easy. I couldn't sleep and kept mulling over what he'd told me.

About 2 am, I had a flash of understanding. Jahred was right. I couldn't see the solution because I was thinking too small. If he was right, my job was the explainer of the vision; the benefits and goals. It was the role of company leadership to embrace the vision and launch their teams into action. And it was their workers' role to figure out how to build and execute the details to match the company's unique needs. I was making this harder than it needed to be. I was looking for something that didn't exist in any book out there. It couldn't exist. Every situation was different. Every company was unique. All I should do is simply explain to the relevant people what our goal was, and let their teams create an optimal path to achieve it. Once I did that, I could declare victory, and move on to the next project as a winner.

I then spent until dawn putting together a presentation explaining the benefits of all that I'd read ... what was in ITIL, why it was good, why it improves the organization, and what types of processes need to be in place to capture all of that greatness for our users. I built the vision and laid out the benefits and the goal; everything leadership needed to be successful.

I was really proud of the thoroughness with which my presentation covered the material. There were no aspects of ITIL I did not explain in the deck of slides. I started the presentation printing and collapsed on the bed to grab at least an hour's sleep before leaving for work.

4: Searching for the Right Place to Start

I chugged two energy drinks in the parking lot at work the next morning. I needed to offset the lack of sleep, and be in top form today.

I stepped into the building and swiped my ID card on the access door with a confident stroke. It was going to be a great day. I was going to present all 21 pages of my presentation to the CIO and her staff. I was confident they would embrace it. This project would make me a winner, and confirm the company had made the right choice by hiring me. I was the new rainmaker and I had the touch.

4: Searching for the Right Place to Start

Tips that would have helped Chris

Best practice, by itself, will not tell you how to implement the solution you need. It won't be detailed enough, or task specific enough, to develop procedures. Think of it as the ideal you aspire to achieve. How you get there is going to be up to you, and the specific situation you face. Don't be afraid to mold it to meet your world.

You can learn from the success of others, even though they come from a different industry. Be careful to ensure that the detail level of the solution you're looking for, matches the detail level they work at. If they provide solutions at a high level of abstraction, their methodology won't provide you with an appropriate path to success.

CHAPTER 5: INVESTIGATING THE WETWARE

My regular Monday morning 8 am one-on-one meeting with Ramesh, was where we went through what I was working on and where it stood. It also provided Ramesh the opportunity to give me his favourite management directive. "What keeps you from having this done already?"

On my way to his office, I'd almost stopped by and asked Jessica's admin to set up a meeting, so I could present my solution to her, and her direct reports, at the earliest opportunity. Maybe it was the lack of sleep, or perhaps it was some cowardly caution on my part, but while waiting for Jessica's admin to finish her phone call and speak to me, I decided to wait until I had cleared it with Ramesh.

He could be such a stickler for the chain of command. I don't think it was a need to micromanage everything, I just think he dreaded having Jessica ask him a question, if he didn't already know the answer. But that was okay. I could wait till he saw it before moving forward. Besides, once Ramesh was onboard, maybe he would help me getting Jessica and the other leaders lined up, too.

Ramesh was smiling and I took that as a good sign.

"I see we had no service outages this weekend, perhaps you are already having an effect," he said and motioned for me to sit down across the desk from him.

He took a long look at me and said, "You look a little like you were working all weekend. Or were you out partying, and now you're trying to recover on the company's time?"

I slapped the pile of color slides down onto his desk.

5: Investigating the Wetware

Pointing to the mound, I said, "Nope, I've got the solution for reducing the number of incidents right here."

I'd made sure the slides were all in appropriate company color format. Each had a tiny image of the company's logo in the corner. I hadn't looked at the full deck as a single unit after printing, but I knew it was a really professional looking set. I'd even taken the time to add some cool animation and transition effects to hold the audience's attention, if I got to project it on a screen. I was really proud of my work.

Ramesh reached across his desk and thumbed the corner of the pile as I said, "I think it's ready to show Jessica and her direct reports, but I wanted to make sure you saw it first."

Distractedly, Ramesh kept scanning through the pages as he mumbled, "Yeah ... thanks." Before stopping and staring directly at me. "Wait a minute, you mean you want to take Jessica's directs, my peers, through this entire encyclopaedia?"

"Only if they want to know how to reduce these incidents," I grinned. "If it were easy and simple, it would have been done long ago. But don't worry. I've distilled it down to these simple concepts. This will just make sure they fully understand the goals and benefits."

With a concerned look, Ramesh added, "But you've got the solution in there, right?"

I nodded. "I've translated the standards into a roadmap of where the leaders need to take their teams, and what the benefits will be. I got some advice from a consultant I know. He is very successful, and works for a high-powered firm that focuses only on Fortune 100 clients."

5: Investigating the Wetware

"And he told you how to do this?"

"It was his concept, but I did the work. And you'll be really proud of me. I got all the advice for free." Ramesh was always on us about watching the budget, so I knew this would connect with him.

"I'm not sure we're talking about the same thing," said Ramesh. "But we'll find out soon enough."

Ramesh fanned the deck several times with his thumb. "How much time are you asking for to present this?"

I'd given plenty of presentations and knew it usually took about two-three minutes per slide, plus time for questions. "Based on my experience, and allowing time to answer all the questions, I'd say about an hour, depending on how many questions they ask. I'll talk fast."

Ramesh slowly shook his head. With a great sigh, he said, "Okay, well we have too many other things to cover today in our one-on-one meeting, but I will give you an hour at our staff meeting tomorrow. You can present it to your peers and see what they say ... unless you were proactive and had already done that."

Ramesh gave me an accusing look, making me realize that I should have gotten feedback from others before talking to him, and he was actually reprimanding me for not doing so. Not a great way to start our one-on-one meeting.

"Normally, I would have, but since I just finished it last night, and know how important this is, I thought it best just to press forward."

"Hmmm. Okay," said Ramesh and pushed the slide deck aside.

5: Investigating the Wetware

We were part way through my ritual chastisement by Ramesh during the one-on-one, when my phone popped up a SEV1 alert. It was one of the few times I was really glad to see something fail; anything to get out of my weekly beating was good. Details began to text in on my phone as we both headed for the War Room.

The business had lost connectivity to a website that allowed customers to buy direct without human intervention. It was a highly profitable tool and generated over 60% of our sales. And now it was off the air; invisible to customers who had money in hand and were dying to give it to us. Needless to say, this upset the sales team greatly, and based on the messages Jessica was forwarding to me from them, they weren't shy about complaining in very graphic scatological terms to everyone they could reach.

By the time we walked into the War Room, Sean had already organized the group and was handing out assignments to get service restored.

Ramesh quickly assessed the action, pulled me aside and said, "You blew it again. It's your job to run these meetings, not Sean's. You should have been here at the beginning and not come in late like this."

I resisted the temptation to remind Ramesh that I was late because I was stuck in a meeting with him, again. I didn't want to get into a finger pointing exercise right now.

"I'm the one bringing the concepts and benefits of the solution," I said. "It's up to people like Sean to develop the execution. Look, he's already off and running. I don't want to slow things down by restarting or micromanaging him."

Ramesh shook his head almost in disbelief. "Is that part of your solution to reducing the number of outages?"

5: Investigating the Wetware

I nodded. "You'll have to wait till you see my presentation. It's all laid out in there."

"I can hardly wait until tomorrow," said Ramesh. "We'll drop the rest of our one-on-one for this week. I have some other more pressing items to deal with. You, or Sean, or someone, needs to get the service restored immediately. I'm leaving the War Room in your hands. Jessica just sent me a text asking me to go apologize to the sales team."

As Ramesh walked away, I was disappointed Jessica hadn't asked me to liaise with sales, but after she saw my solution things would be different. For now, I needed to stay focused on getting the service restored and this incident closed.

Sean was standing at one end of the room, directly in front of the whiteboard. It was covered in cryptic network diagrams and bulleted lists of what may have caused the outage. As I watched him run the meeting, I realized how impressive Sean was at managing these events and resolving incidents in the traditional manner.

There was no question that he was in charge and everyone in the room seemed happy with it. There was none of the usual e-mail reading, chatting, or other activities people do when they are bored, or unconnected, with a meeting. They were all focused on him.

I watched as Sean assigned some critical tasks to himself, and some key players, while giving others supporting roles. He was not only the process leader; he was also the task leader. Actually, there wasn't any process. When working via a process you are always aware that there is a beginning, activities and an end. But in this world; Sean's

5: Investigating the Wetware

world, there was only this Zen-like focus on the current moment.

Priorities were crystal clear to everyone in the room; all other activities were secondary. The level of urgency was clear; get the service back online and do it now. Issues of turf, conflict, or finger pointing, never came up. They were irrelevant with service to the business down. Critical situations called for a superhero to step in and resolve them for the good of the company.

I didn't like the idea of managing incidents by superhero, but watching this group in action, I could almost see Sean wearing a cape while bringing order and safety to the environment. I just couldn't help wondering what would happen if there were multiple incidents at the same time.

After all the assignments had been handed out and people began restoring the service, I wandered away and headed back to my cube. My presence was redundant and I was still a little groggy from all the work and lack of sleep over the weekend.

After I got the message on my phone that service had been restored, I wandered over to Sean's desk with my deck of slides. With his experience, he'd probably be one of the individuals leadership relied on to develop and execute the tasks necessary to achieve the benefits from these best practices. So it only made sense to give him a peak at it beforehand.

"What did you think about the way we handled that problem?" asked Sean. "That's how we do it old-school. It's efficient and effective."

"You did a great job restoring service after the incident. I don't know if we can say it qualifies as a problem yet.

5: Investigating the Wetware

There is a difference between the two, and it's important to be consistent in language, so we all understand each other," I said. "If we aren't consistent in our terminology, the resulting miscommunications may create disruptions in the delivery of our services to the business."

"Don't be such a wonk," said Sean dismissively. "Go ask the business if they thought the loss of their e-commerce site was a problem or not."

"But at least you collected information on the incident so we could evaluate it, to see if it should be part of problem management," I said hopefully, repeating the phrases I'd learned over the weekend. "You know; categorization, diagnosis and workarounds. Things like that."

Sean scowled and rolled his eyes. "Why bother? Knowing that doesn't help you resolve it any faster. The people qualified to resolve these types of problems know. They have that information in their head from experience. There is no need to fill out another useless form. Don't be such a bureaucrat. Go ahead and test me. Ask me about any problem I've had to deal with. I can tell you whatever you need to know to restore service if something similar occurs again. I can even tell you its symptoms, so we can start fixing it sooner."

He still didn't get the difference between problems and incidents. "And if you're not available the next time when it happens?" I asked. "What happens then?"

"What we have always done, we call on some other experienced wetware."

"Wetware?"

5: Investigating the Wetware

Sean laughed. "You have no imagination at all, do you? You've heard of hardware ... equipment and devices. You've heard of software ... instructions in a computer's memory. Well, wetware is people. We're over 60% water ... so wet-ware. It's like liveware or meatware. They're all the same thing. Get it? If I'm not available, there are several other long-term employees who know how everything works." With a laugh he added, "Of course, they're not as good as me, but they'll do."

I shook my head. "You need to get more sleep. Or else get out among normal people a little more."

"You miss my point. I know ITIL. Just because I don't use it, or like it, doesn't mean I'm ignorant. I don't dismiss things out of hand until I understand them. And I really understand ITIL, probably better than you do. I've even got a certificate somewhere for a class I took. It was the most wasted week of my life."

Now I was getting confused. I'd seen a lot of great things in the ITIL standards, but I watched Sean organize a solution to the service disruption and get the business back online in very little time. "So you think your approach is better than best practices that have been vetted worldwide, and are in use by thousands of companies?"

"You're missing the point again. Your lack of hands-on operational experience is showing," he said. "ITIL, eTOM, ISO20000 and all those other standards, do a nice job of putting all the concepts into a framework, but they're way too academic. They read like talking to a consultant. They're not focused on the needs of the people executing the tasks at hand; the worker bees. They make it so much more complex than it needs to be. It's as if they are trying to exclude anyone who hasn't spent years studying it, and

5: Investigating the Wetware

the only way you can understand it is by having some anointed and certified specialist interpret for you.

That's the same trap traditional IT fell into, where IT people were the sacred priests, and users had to come to us for interpretation and instruction. All that theory is great. But that's the point. It's all just theoretical knowledge. It's not tangible in a way that immediately helps people who have to execute day-to-day operations."

Sean picked up a marker and began drawing pictures on the small whiteboard in his cube to illustrate his points. "Our business partners don't care about all the life cycle stuff. They don't want to know anything about what goes on in IT behind the curtain. For all they care, we could have a million monkeys throwing darts to make any decision, and we configure hardware by randomly connecting things until something works."

When his board was filled with pictures of monkeys and servers with circles and arrows connecting them, he began gesturing at the pictures with the marker. "None of that matters to them. All they desire is for us to give them what they want, when they need it, at a cost they can afford, and to not break anything else while doing it. More than that just confuses and irritates them. That's the mistake people make who never get beyond the standards. They think the business really cares if we call something an incident or a problem, or what the seven steps are to achieving some other theoretical concept. All the business cares about is meeting their objectives. That is what they get paid for. And they count on us to provide services that allow them to do just that. Standards are just high-level lists of what helped some other IT teams do a better job, in some other place, at some other time."

5: Investigating the Wetware

Finally, Sean threw his marker into the tray at the bottom of the whiteboard and sat down behind his desk. "You gotta remember ... IT people are planning engineers with the luxury of a multi-year time horizon. People on the business side are often forced to focus quarter to quarter, program to program, due to competition, or the economy, or a million other things. Sure they think about the out years, but they know that if they don't make the current goals, the out years won't matter. The world is too dynamic for them to waste a lot of time working with IT on life cycle and continual improvement for the out years."

"Like I said, do you have a better alternative?" I asked. "Or should we just wait for the business to tell us what to do, and then run in circles until it's done and never worry about stopping incidents from recurring?"

"I bet you'd call the way I handled the outage today as not best practice. We didn't collect any information about ... "

I cut him off, "And so it will happen again and again. Each time it will disrupt service to our business partners. You can't tell me they don't care about reducing the number of times it happens."

"That's one of the misconceptions IT has about the business," he responded. "They don't expect IT to be perfect. Don't pay attention to all the yelling they do. It's how they work. They expect stuff to break. They understand that. But what they worry about is how long it will be down. The more complicated the systems are, the more often they're going to break; the more possible points of failure that exist. And when it does break, the IT wetware knows the fastest possible way to fix it. Stuff will always break. You can't prevent that from happening.

5: Investigating the Wetware

Maybe you can in the perfect world of standards, but in the real world ... never."

"So, you're suggesting that management by superhero is the best way we can support the business? Don't we owe them more than that?"

"Don't be so idealistic, Chris. We owe them a service level. How we do that is none of their business. That's why all that life cycle, continual improvement, vague, academic mumbo-jumbo, is just another way for tool vendors and consultants to set up shop here. Why do you think it's written at such an abstract level? It's not real world with real people and real situations. Try giving those books to someone who's got to deliver on a day-to-day basis, and see if they can find a specific set of tasks in there that will help them. If they want to make those standards more useful, they should crawl out of their ivory towers and try living in the real world, instead of selling concepts to executives. I bet they would change their tune real quick, and drop the academic perspective for some reality-based answers. Every time I hear one of those consultants come in and sell leadership on the benefits of some vision and then take off, leaving us to figure out how to actually make it work, I want to punch them."

"Well, don't hold back Sean. I think you are being much too shy and demur."

"Which would you rather have; a group of rookies and a set of instructions and processes, or actual experts who had done it so often they could solve the problem with their eyes closed, in a fraction of the time? Ask the business that question and you'll have your answer. The superhero model works because it keeps the business running, and it works much better than a bunch of abstract ideas."

5: Investigating the Wetware

Sean threw a wad of paper at me and laughed. "Remember, you can't argue with the company superheroes. We've got capes and special powers."

I laughed along with him. It helped bring the conversation back down from such an intense, almost confrontational, level. I couldn't tell if Sean was serious or not, but I still knew he was wrong.

Everything I'd learned, and everything I used in my presentation, said he was wrong. He'd just been doing things one way so long, he couldn't see any other way to work. For a moment, I had an uneasy feeling that maybe there were some tiny truths buried deep in what he said. But I wasn't going to deconstruct his rant right now. In fact, I wasn't even going to show him my presentation. I had too much faith in what I'd already learned and my presentation.

The next day I was the first one into the room for Ramesh's staff meeting. I double and triple checked the projector and my laptop, making sure there would be no mechanical problems. I paced the room, getting comfortable with the space.

When the clock clicked past the meeting start time, and I was the only one in the room, I began to nervously check the time and location again, to confirm I was in the right place. This was an important presentation and I didn't want to mess it up by being in the wrong place, at the wrong time.

Slowly, people started to wander in, filling the room with animated conversations. They ranged from complaints about work, to sports scores, to what was on television last night. I stayed out of the conversations. My focus was on observing the other people to get a sense of their mood, and

5: Investigating the Wetware

planning what I would need to do to focus their attention on my presentation.

Ramesh was the last one into the room. He was finishing a call with Jessica as he stomped in and threw himself down in a chair. Judging by the scowl on his face, it had not been a pleasant call. He skipped his usual agenda and as promised, quickly set the stage for my presentation and then turned it over to me.

I set the pile of hard copies on the table beside me. When a couple of people started to reach for them, I said, "I'm going to hand these out at the end. Right now I want you to focus on our discussion." I could tell by the look on their faces that they weren't happy, but I didn't want any distractions.

"I'll bet all the pages in the presentations are blank. That's why you don't want to hand them out. The pile is just for dramatic effect," said Molly to the room. She got a good laugh from everyone, but unfortunately, it defocused people from the message at hand.

I stood silently at the head of the conference room table until the laughter had died down, and then counted out a few more seconds. I loved how that moment of quiet before a presentation brought everyone into sync, as they wondered what was next.

When the silence became almost too much, I began working through all 21 slides in the presentation deck. I knew that to sell this audience, I needed to give them not just the "What" of the standards, but also the "Why". So I had structured the presentation as a flow, first identifying the core elements of incident and problem management, then the benefits from applying each one together as a

5: Investigating the Wetware

group, and finally, how they needed to understand these practices and turn them into specific actions relevant to their team.

As I started into the deck, I was actually grateful to Ramesh for insisting I present to his staff first. It gave me a chance to pretend they were executive leadership and test out my delivery. I made notes as I spoke, on changes on the delivery, to consider for the final presentation to Jessica.

I'd given a lot of presentations and was pretty good at it. I'd never had trouble keeping my audience engaged and attentive, but by the fifth slide, Molly had begun to thumb her phone, checking e-mail. Rose had waited until the eighth slide to open her laptop and start typing. Determined not to let them get to me, I pressed on. It would be their loss. By the time I got to the end, everyone was working on something else. Although I was pleased that Ramesh seemed to still be engaged and I'd made it through without any interruptions from the audience.

"Any questions?" I asked, as I turned off the projector and handed out the printed copies.

The room was silent except for the click of keys, until Ramesh looked around the room and asked the team, "So what did you think of the information Chris presented? Do you think we can use it to solve our problems?"

I winced. Clearly, Ramesh had missed the key points on slide six about the difference between problems and incidents, and the importance of consistent terminology. I made a mental note to stress that more when I spoke to the senior leadership.

Everyone stopped their activity and looked at Ramesh; not at me, or the color hard copies of the slide decks I'd given

5: Investigating the Wetware

them. Actually, I was a little disappointed that no one seemed to be reading the copies now that I was done with the presentation.

Finally, Montrell picked up the slide deck and stared at it in his hand, as if trying to judge its weight. "It looks very professional, Chris. There is a lot of material in here. Perhaps too much for me to grasp all at once. Can't you make it a little simpler; a little more relevant to my day-to-day activities? Perhaps I missed it, but I don't know what you are asking me to do. I don't know if you want my help, my approval, or if you're just informing me about something."

I smiled. That confirmed I had the right presentation for the executives. They would never ask that kind of question. They had the perspective to understand the benefits and would see the need to engage their teams to identify the tactical solutions once I'd presented this transformational analysis.

Montrell waved the slide deck at me and said, "I guess I'm not as smart as you are, Chris. If you say this will help us reduce the impact of incidents on our delivery of services to the business, then by all means press on and full speed ahead. Do whatever you have to do. It would just help me if you could add a summary for the rest of us. Just tell us what you plan to do, and what you want us to do. We have too many other demands on us to try to learn everything you've presented."

Everyone else nodded.

"Yeah, a summary ... maybe bullets of the top four or five things we need to execute on a single sheet of paper," said Molly. "I trust you Chris. I don't need to know the specifics

5: Investigating the Wetware

of everything you are doing. Just give me the high points of what you're going to ask my team to execute, so I can back you up intelligently if anyone on my team has questions."

"Perhaps I wasn't direct enough about what was expected of you," I said. "What I have laid out here is the fundamental processes that must be in place in order for us to reduce the number of incidents we experience, and the list of benefits from doing so. Everyone has a role in that. My task is to translate the conceptual model ... the best practice standards ... into our common experience. Your role will be to identify the steps you need to take to align with those standards, and work with your teams to develop a plan to execute them."

Montrell gave me a puzzled look. "So you explain the theory to me and then walk away ... leaving me to figure out what to do and then do it?"

I nodded. "Except, I'm not going anywhere. I will still be available to explain any points of confusion about the standards and the expectations they set."

Molly shook her head and stuffed the deck into her pack. "Oh, I get it now. Thanks a lot. I'll take a look at it."

"Thanks, Chris," said Ramesh. "I think that is all the time we have for this week. I'll catch up with each of you during our one-on-one meetings."

As people started packing up and leaving, Ramesh asked me to stay behind for a moment.

After everyone was gone and I finished packing up the last of my material, Ramesh said, "So Chris, how do you think it went? Did it go as you had planned?"

5: Investigating the Wetware

I shook my head. "Actually, I'm a little disappointed that they didn't pick up more of the material and start to identify what they needed to do to implement and execute their portion of these processes. I thought they had a broader business perspective. But maybe that's the difference between them and executives. I can't be too critical of them. I think once leadership lays out the path, they will start to understand and turn this into executable tasks."

"I've thought about this a lot," said Ramesh. "After seeing your presentation, and based on my experience, I think you will get a better reception from senior leadership if you have some successes to point at. So why don't you keep working to turn your solution into some successes before scheduling any time with Jessica or the CEO?"

"Actually, I was planning to go ahead and set something up with Jessica right away. There is no reason to single-thread this. I'd rather attack on a number of fronts at the same time."

Ramesh shook his head. "Let me be more direct. First show some success with your approach in terms of driving down incidents, and then we'll talk to Jessica and ask for her help. Under no circumstances should you schedule, or conduct, a review of this with Jessica, or the other executives, without some successes and my approval. Is that clear? You'll only get one shot with them, and with some level of impact on outages, you will have a much better chance at success."

"But why? It's all right there. Surely you see that."

"It's not a debate, Chris. Show me some buy-in from my peers, and some reduction in outages first," said Ramesh as he stood up and began walking out of the room. "Trust me on this. I'm only looking out for your best interests."

5: Investigating the Wetware

He stopped at the doorway and closed the door. Quietly he said, "And here's some important advice to be kept between you and me. Don't pay so much attention to Sean. He always looks out for what is good for Sean, above all else. That's how he's been able to stay employed here for so long. He doesn't always have your best interests in mind, but Jessica listens to him a lot. So while it is important to be on good terms with him so he says positive things to Jessica about you, do not trust him. Do you understand?"

I nodded.

"Good," he said. "This conversation never happened."

After Ramesh was gone, I slumped down into a chair in the empty room. I wasn't concerned about his comments on Sean. I was mad at being held back by him. Maybe Ramesh now saw me as a threat to his job. Perhaps he was afraid that if I were successful in reducing the number of incidents, I would be such a hero that Jessica would give me his job. But I couldn't go against his direct order without risking my job. Now I was determined to beat Ramesh at his own game; to meet his criteria and force him into the meeting with the executives. I was not going to let him stop me now, no matter how much he was afraid of me.

I turned off the light and closed the door as I headed back to my cube. I walked by Sean's empty cube and Ramesh's parting warning about Sean came back. I wondered if there was any truth to what he'd told me. More importantly, why did he tell me that, and what should I do with that information?

5: Investigating the Wetware

Tips that would have helped Chris

Sell your ideas from the bottom up first, and then from the top down. Always make sure you are aligned with the people who will have to live with your proposal day-to-day, before you take it to their leadership. This will help flush out any weaknesses in your proposal and build organizational support.

If you focus your ideas on a narrow scope, you will make them easier to understand and communicate. The objective is not to impress the audience with how much you know. The goal is to draw their attention to a single issue, how you propose to deal with it, and the benefits of your solution.

The best ITSM implementation is not the one that most correctly follows the ITIL terminology or process designs. The best implementation is the one that does the most for the users. Purity of compliance with ITIL terminology and process flow is not worth anything if service to the users is not improved.

CHAPTER 6: MANAGING SERVICE OUTAGES

Hiu was manager of the network team, and from the initial looks at the data I'd seen, a lot of the incidents had his team involved in some way to resolve them. It didn't necessarily mean his team was responsible for them. It just meant he had great visibility of what restored the service.

The references had been pretty clear. With only incident management, no matter how good we got at resolving outages, we could never reduce the number of incidents. That was where problem management made all the difference. I was convinced of that, it had to be part of the solution, too. I needed the help of Hiu's team if I were going to be able to get problem management off the ground. The question in my mind was whether I could convince him to be part of the solution.

I needed to find a way to get him on my side. I'd been told that Hiu was a big fan of churrascarias; those rodizio style restaurants with roving passadores; servers who come to your table with meat on skewers and carved them to your order. It was a good place to meet on business. You could set up a slow pace to the meal, making it almost as good as golf for locking in plenty of time for talk.

"So I figure you must have a reason for buying me lunch besides wanting to spend an hour in my company, right?" said Hiu as he worked on his lunch. "After seeing the unceremonious way they bounced Sarah out for being unable to halt the outages, I guess you must be the next sacrificial offering. They've thrown you under the bus, but it hasn't arrived yet. If you're quick enough, you can

6: Managing Service Outages

escape, but otherwise, you'll follow her out the door. Am I right?"

I didn't answer. Somehow admitting to my own risky situation was not the kind of pressure I needed. "I'm still kind of new here. Did you know Sarah well?"

Hiu nodded. "We both started about the same time. It was too bad she got treated that way. She'd done a lot of good things while she was here. I guess the only thing that counts is what you've done for them today."

"Are you at risk in your role? How's the last thing you did?" I asked. I needed to know how motivated Hiu was if I asked him to change the way he was doing business.

"Given that I'm probably one of two or three people in the whole company who know how the entire network works, I'd say I'm pretty close to indispensible ... at least more than you are," he laughed.

I shrugged my shoulders. "I guess that's one way to look at it. All depends on whether or not the number of incidents goes down. You know, those things that get you paged in the middle of the night and on weekends. If they don't decrease, no one is safe."

"Actually, I don't mind getting paged. Neither does my team." Hiu leaned across the table, poking the air between us with his knife. "It's a real rush when you're responding to business outages. The company is in crisis and everyone is counting on you to step in and work your magic to make everything right. I mean, who doesn't love showing off their skills? Besides, the business is very appreciative towards those that solve those problems quickly. They definitely do not forget your name. You wouldn't believe all the free lunches, swag and sports tickets they push my

6: Managing Service Outages

way in gratitude. And when we go for a week or two without an outage, they're even more grateful."

Hiu stopped and put his knife down. "And here's some advice to you from someone who's been around for a while. Nothing is better for you at review time than a big pile of certificates of excellence, and appreciation from our business partners. That always impresses leaders and ensures you get a nice raise."

I didn't even bother to try and explain the difference between incidents and problems at this point. That would be later. Right now I had to find something in his view of the world to grab onto; anything that would make him think about helping me. I asked the obvious. "Don't you think they wouldn't be even more grateful if you prevented those outages?"

"Not a chance, Chris. I know that's what they teach you in those ITIL classes. That may be the way academics and executives think, but you've got to look at it from the perspective of their operational teams; the people who get their hands dirty delivering results for business operations. If nothing ever breaks, IT is invisible. We become a utility. How many times have you called up the electric company and thanked them because the power didn't go off at your house yesterday? People only value things they struggle for. Things that don't kill you, make you stronger, and things that cost you dearly, are always valued more highly. If you make it too easy and give it to them for free, they will never appreciate it."

"So it's about doing what makes the business grateful to you personally, rather than doing what's right for the business, even though you may not get credit for it?" I asked, trying to see how far he was going down this path.

6: Managing Service Outages

"They aren't exclusive, Chris. You're thinking like an abstract academic; like this is a perfect world. In the real world you are never going to get rid of outages. Something will always happen. If you're not ready for that, you shouldn't be in IT. And while those outages are regrettable, and I wish they didn't happen, the fact they do, simply reinforces to the business that the money they give to IT is important and well spent."

Logic was not going to work with Hiu. There was no way I could change his beliefs in the timeframe I needed. Perhaps after he saw how the business reacted to making IT almost invisible, as he put it, because there were so few incidents, he might change. But I needed him to start systematically collecting data on incidents before I had any hope of getting problem management off the ground, and I was convinced that was the only way I could generate some successes and get in front of Jessica with my solution.

"Interesting. I'd never thought of it that way. So how do you identify to the business and leadership all the times you stepped up and went beyond the norm?" I asked.

"I can usually remember them, especially the recent ones."

"I can see that," I said, as the passadore started slicing some roasted, yet unidentifiable hunk of flesh on a skewer, planted firmly on the table between us. "I just think it would be more impressive if they had a context; you know, how many there were in total, what happened and why? It would make a powerful statement about how much work you're actually doing for them. I know if I were in your place, that's what I'd do."

6: Managing Service Outages

"All that tracking would be a pain. I just want to get in, fix it, and get out. More than that is way too much. They are not as fixated on the detail as someone in IT might be."

"Maybe I can help," I offered. "Our ticketing system already has the ability to track that. All it needs is a few other pieces of data, and it can produce all kinds of reports about how valuable your service has been to the business. It's nothing new, just noting at the time of the incident the same stuff you carry in your head, like what you did to fix it, what caused it, which part of the business was impacted. You know all that already. It's nothing new. I can show your team how to do it if you want? It's up to you. But it would definitely give you a bigger list of valuable accomplishments to impress the business with."

Hiu looked long and hard at me, and then smiled. "You know, Chris, when you first started here I figured you to be a bureaucratic jerk, whose sole mission in life was to slow us down. I guess I was wrong. Maybe tracking some of this data would be worth doing, so we can get credit for everything we do. But if I get a single complaint from my team, we stop it, right?"

I nodded. "Yep."

"Then it's a deal. Come lay it out for my team on Thursday at my staff meeting. And remember, if anybody complains, it's over."

"Thanks," I said. "I appreciate the opportunity. I'm sure they will see the value in it, just as you do."

"As far as all that ITIL standards stuff goes," said Hiu. "Let me give you one bit of advice. I deal with a lot of networking standards, so I understand what they are like. Always make sure you adapt the standards to the situation.

6: Managing Service Outages

Don't force the situation to meet the standard. You may not get that golden city on the hill the standard is focused on, but you'll get something that gives you 80% of what you need. Don't try to get to the end state on day one. Make progress your goal, rather than your ideal state."

Hiu stood up and pushed his chair in. "Now, where is that dessert buffet and espresso bar. I need some serious sugar and caffeine to balance out all this protein."

The meeting with Hiu's team went much better than I had hoped. It was helped because I'd visited each person individually before meeting with them as a group. That allowed me to ferret out their concerns. And it probably didn't hurt that I had taken Hiu's advice and made sure I could craft and be happy with a process they could live with, too. That made them feel like they had some skin in the game.

Initially, I felt guilty about compromising the standards I learned. When I read the books and studied the standards, it seemed all very cut and dried. Focus on the standard and how you can make reality fit it. There didn't seem to be any leeway to deviate from the standards and still be compliant. Settling for anything less than best practice seemed like failure. Somehow, adequate practice just didn't have the same ring to it.

But while working with the Network team, I realized Hiu was absolutely right. If you tried to force fit high-level concepts into reality without taking the local landscape into account, the best you could possibly hope for was minimal task compliance. Anyone could do that with sufficient executive clout behind them.

6: Managing Service Outages

Hiu had helped me realize that processes, or any other behavior change, only succeeds and matures if people embrace them. Mere compliance was not enough. The real art to implementing behavior change was in understanding the needs of the process participants, and creating an intermediate state they could live with, which at the same time would move you toward the ideal state you desired. We might never get there in my lifetime, but my goal was reduction in outages, not elimination.

Once I realized that, it became clear I wasn't so much concerned about the purity and perfect alignment with the ITIL standards. Instead, I was focused on getting something … anything started, no matter how ugly. I was going to start small and messy, and grow the maturity and completeness over time. But above all, I was going to morph to meet reality, and not ask reality to shift to conform.

I knew this was the right path, because by the time I was done, Hiu's team was eager to participate, demanding to know when we would start. Once I had cracked that code to getting acceptance of my ideas, aligning the rest of the teams was easy. In fact, when they found out that Hiu's team was onboard with me, they began to clamour for participation.

It was interesting how competitive the technical teams were when it came to performance. Perhaps it had something to do with the inherent role measurement plays in technical domains. I didn't care. I was too pleased at how knowing other teams were getting onboard, made selling the other teams on the ideas so much easier.

I'd even backed off on trying to end the superhero era and push Sean into a corner. There was no need to. Once the

6: Managing Service Outages

teams had started using the ticketing system to log some of the data surrounding incidents, it didn't matter. They were pulling in all the data I needed. As long as the information about the incident was collected, I could live with superheroes. And if the goal of incident management was to get the business back online as quickly as possible, then maybe there was some value in a superhero approach for the time being.

My excitement about getting incident data entered into the database lasted only until I actually started to work with the data. The ticketing tool was an incredibly complex database a software engineer had built one weekend several years ago. She'd apparently tried to replicate the full functionality of ticket databases she worked with elsewhere. Leadership lauded her for it because it was free, and they didn't have to use it. The technical teams loved it because it had been built in-house and confirmed that the company's technical teams were better than any on the outside. And of course, they hadn't been using it either.

Of course, the developer had long since left the company. Her code was idiosyncratic, unstructured and undocumented. Most of the fields were useless, except in a much more mature environment. Anyone who'd tried to make changes to the database usually ended up breaking something else. The database didn't record very much, just some basic information, and most of that was contained in free-text fields. It was hardly the right way to do it. But then again, in a superhero based world where you never worried about preventing incidents, who needed a lot of categorizing, or sorting of information?

Everyone was entering data in different ways, and apparently in cryptic code only understandable to

6: Managing Service Outages

themselves. The only way I could make sense out of the notes was to wade through each individual ticket. Usually I ended up calling the person who made the notes and asking them to translate. The ironic part was that often even they could not make sense of their own notes.

I was deep into trying to understand the SEV1 tickets over the last 45 days when Ramesh walked into my cube. Before he could speak, my phone alerted for another SEV1.

"Looks like you are failing to shut these outages down," he said with a scowl. "I haven't seen any reduction in outages since you started working on this."

"It takes time," I mumbled, as I texted Sean to ask if he was going to lead the War Room. "We've done a lot to improve the process. It just takes time to have effect."

"Actually, what you've done after all these weeks is to get incident responders to fill out forms after the incident," said Ramesh. "If that's how ITIL is going to reduce outages, then I'm not very impressed with either its theory, or your practice. Something has to change, and you'd better figure it out soon. I doubt Jessica has a lot more patience."

Ramesh took one look at the piles of paper on my desk and said, "What a mess. No wonder you don't know what is going on. I want to see your quantitative evidence of how our incident situation has improved, by tomorrow."

Just then Sean responded to my text with a message that he was busy elsewhere and I'd need to go manage the outage myself this time. This was going to be an ugly day.

6: Managing Service Outages

Tips that would have helped Chris

Not everyone shares your likes or dislikes. Many IT people like the adrenaline of late-night paging and War Rooms. You need to find a common goal as the basis for building relationships, before you can work out a solution and gain commitment.

Try to build new processes, such that it does not increase the workload on the technical SMEs. You want it to ultimately allow them to focus on their technical discipline, not filling out forms. If you have to add bureaucracy to their workflow, make sure they understand why it is important and whom it benefits. And above all, make sure they have a hand in designing it.

CHAPTER 7: TIME TO REFOCUS

I couldn't believe the numbers.

I checked them three times, but it always came out the same. Over the last 90 days, the number of incidents had remained almost constant. There had been a few swings between teams, but the total wasn't statistically different than it had been before I started.

All that work; all the effort I had invested was for nothing. I had done my best to get the incident management team to gather enough data so they could identify how to prevent repeat disruptions to the service. There always seemed to be another incident that got in the way of them spending the time they needed to get the answer and make it happen.

I could hear Ramesh now, and no matter how I envisioned it; the last words out of his mouth were always, "You're Fired."

As if to reinforce my utter failure, my phone lit up with another SEV1 incident. Several clusters of stores in the Western Region had lost the ability to operate their cash drawers. That meant no customer transactions, payments, or cash receipts. Needless to say, sales were nearly apoplectic.

This was the fourth time in the last two months it had happened. I knew the symptoms by heart. The solution was simple and worked consistently; reboot the servers controlling the cash drawers in the stores. Unfortunately, by the time they were in this state, direct access to the physical server itself from a crash cart in the data centre, was the only way to fully power cycle the platform to get the server working again.

7: Time to Refocus

I wanted to let my business contact know we were on top of it and that the store cash drawers would be back online within 30 minutes. But before I could message her, she dropped a text on my phone asking if we had rebooted the servers yet. And then added a note that during the flight to New York yesterday she read an article about how Cloud Computing would prevent this type of thing from ever happening, and wondered why we hadn't thought of doing something like that for them.

I couldn't believe it. The incident situation was now so out of control that our business partners knew the symptoms and how to restore the service, as well as IT did. They were even telling us how to redesign our services. I picked up one of the ITIL books and threw it against the wall of my cube.

As if on cue, Ramesh showed up a few minutes later looking for the results. I lied and told him they weren't ready yet. I was too upset to have a discussion about why incidents had not decreased, despite all of the efforts we had put into them, and I didn't think I could take getting fired right this minute. I needed more time to put an explanation together, along with a plan of action to fix things, so I would at least have a chance at keeping my job. If the job market had been any better, I probably would have resigned myself to the fact that the task was impossible and just quit. Better to go out on your under terms than be tossed out. Besides, not every task can be successfully completed. Some were just too unrealistic to achieve.

Ramesh picked up the ITIL book lying on the floor where I'd thrown it. He sat down opposite me and pushed the

7: Time to Refocus

book across the desk toward me. "Looks like you dropped this."

"Chris," said Ramesh. "This is more than just a social call. I've been off-site with the rest of IT leadership working on our strategic and tactical plans for the future. We discussed your recommendation that we staff separate problem management and incident management leaders, by allowing you to hire a problem manager to supplement the incident manager."

The new incident manager hadn't been a hire. I'd been assigned Darren, by Ramesh. This was Darren's third role in 18 months. Unfortunately, I'd heard that he didn't get moved because he was a superstar that crushed objectives and led like a hero. He was related by marriage to one of the members of the Board of Directors. When his own entrepreneurial business venture had gone under a couple of years ago, his employment by the company had been arranged. What he lacked in knowledge and experience, he made up for in enthusiasm. He did have one highly honed skill, aside from marrying well. He was very good at slapping together a chaotic jumble of work, then declaring victory and moving on. Usually, his manager would support and commend his work for the simple reason that it was the only way to have him go work for someone else.

For some reason, Darren and Sean seemed to connect like brothers from different mothers. Sean had taken him under his tutelage, and spent countless hours helping him actually master the role of incident manager. So I let Sean mentor him, despite Sean's superhero tendencies. That freed me up to concentrate on problem management, and actually got me some credit as the person who had figured out the right niche for Darren in the company. Darren actually seemed to

7: Time to Refocus

like the job, with all its chaotic adrenaline and constantly changing focus. No outage seemed to exceed his attention span.

It was good to see Darren grow, and maybe even find a place for himself. But there was no way he had the personality, or focus, to be the problem manager. He didn't have that questioning attention to detail, and dogged pursuit of the answer a problem manager needs. Asking him to do both jobs was a recipe for disaster.

"I know I'm still kinda new here, Ramesh," I said. "But shouldn't I have had the chance to make my case to them directly?"

"It wouldn't have been appropriate. In light of the tight economy and our financial goals for the future, leadership needs to be able to have a frank discussion full of give and take that involves both potential new hires, as well as the capabilities of existing employees. If you were at the meeting, it might inhibit leaders from the open and frank discussions we needed to have in order to optimize our resources, to best meet the needs of the business. There is just too much personal and confidential information discussed. Besides, it wouldn't be fair to people being discussed. That is privileged information."

Ramesh sat down on the other side of my desk. "But don't worry; I made a vigorous presentation and defence of your recommendation as an IDLE best practice."

7: Time to Refocus

"That's ITIL, Ramesh. Information Technology Infrastructure Library®[2]. ITIL."

Ramesh shook his head and waved his hands at me. "Don't worry. It was for a group of leaders ... people focused on the content, not on the peripheral aspects of the name."

I resisted the urge to push it further, and pulled out the personnel requisition and job description for the problem manager. I pushed them across the desk to Ramesh.

"I appreciate your support and efforts. Congratulations on getting them to approve this. When can I get it posted? I really need this person on board, so we can make some headway."

Ramesh fanned the documents and pushed them back across the table to me. "The IT leadership has decided to postpone the staffing you recommended. They decided the positions of incident manager and problem manager are so similar, that one person should cover them both."

"Didn't you show them my analysis supporting the recommendation?" I pulled the slide deck from my files and pushed it across the table toward Ramesh.

Ramesh fanned through the slides. "Although the case we made was well-reasoned and appropriate, when compared to some of the other staffing needs, it seemed like redundant positions at a time when we do not have the resources to fill all the critical roles IT needs."

He pushed the slide deck back at me. "In fact, a solid case was made that separating these roles would cause a loss of

---

[2] IT Infrastructure Library® is a registered trade mark of the Cabinet Office.

7: Time to Refocus

information about key elements during the handoff from incident manager to problem manager. There was strong consensus among the leadership that based on their extensive experience, the incident team was best equipped to determine how to prevent the incidents from recurring again, because they were closest to the facts. The idea of bringing another group in to make that determination made no sense and would be counter-productive."

"Leadership has zero experience with problem management," I protested. "Did you tell them that it is precisely because the incident team is so close to the event, that you need a problem management team? The incident team is too close to the immediate events to see the patterns," I said.

"It was all discussed at length in a very open and frank discussion, before leadership reached its conclusions. Jessica had spent a great deal of her time soliciting input from a number of employees directly involved in the restoration of service after incidents."

"So the answer is no?"

Ramesh nodded. "I am truly sorry. But out of respect for all that has been accomplished so far, leadership did agree that if the critical headcount needs get filled and additional resources become available, they will absolutely reconsider it without prejudice ... provided we can demonstrate a way to prevent loss of information during the handoff from one team to the other. You should be proud that they gave you that strong endorsement. Till then, please integrate the two activities under the incident manager and get the number of service disruptions down. Everyone is counting on you."

7: Time to Refocus

Ramesh smiled, stood up, and just before he walked away said, "I'm sure that in light of all of the conversations we have had in the past about influencers, you can understand leadership's discovery and thought process."

Ramesh then walked away without saying goodbye. As soon as he was gone, I picked up the ITIL book he'd returned to me and threw it against the wall again. How did leadership expect me to succeed if they wouldn't support me? Oh sure, when I'd asked them, everyone had been supportive and willing to invest in the staffing needed, because it was essential to the success of the company. But when it came to investing in problem management, or their own pet projects, it was no contest. I guess I had been naive in my discussions. The reality was that no matter how much they told me they were supporting me, when things got tough, they'd toss me aside if it suited their purposes better. And was Ramesh's allusion at the end to Sean true, or just another diversion? I wasn't sure it mattered anymore.

Fortunately, I didn't have time to wallow in frustration and self-pity. There was a problem management meeting in two days and I needed to find Darren and let him know about his promotion from incident manager to problem and incident manager. It was time for his education to begin.

The problem management meeting started on time, but Darren was missing the meeting ... again. Over the last few weeks, since he'd become the joint incident and problem manager, he hadn't missed a single incident restoration gathering, but his attendance at problem management meetings had been low, and his working with the technical teams on remediation plans had become almost non-existent.

7: Time to Refocus

It wasn't that he didn't know what to do. He'd set up the meetings and have plans and objectives for each meeting all laid out. I had trained him well, and I had to give him credit for executing. It may have been the most focused and organized thing he'd ever done in his entire life.

But every time there was an incident, he'd drop all of his problem work and scurry off to restore the service. The frustrating part was that Ramesh had been given a lot of very positive feedback from the business about Darren's performance. It appeared that the business was really focused on the current moment, and as long as service disruptions were being addressed quickly, they felt it was an improvement.

It just made no sense to me. I was still confused as to why the business couldn't see that by investing in problem management, we could reduce the number of incidents. And with our better response capabilities in incident management, we could really produce a much better service environment for them. But the biggest disappointment was in the IT department, where no one seemed very interested in reducing the number of incidents, as long as the business wasn't complaining. They seemed to believe that incidents were the thing that provided tangible proof of the value of IT. Prevention made them uneasy because they couldn't count the number of crises they'd prevented. Restoration gave them a sense of worth and contribution that could be measured. Perhaps Sean had been right after all. All that mattered here was quick treatment of the symptoms. No one wanted the cure.

I sent Darren a text and a phone message, but with no response. I started the meeting without him, because of all the SEV1s we'd had in the past week. We needed to assess

7: Time to Refocus

which of them needed to go through the full root cause and remediation process, and which were better handled on an observational basis.

Darren arrived about 20 minutes late, an energy drink in his hand. "Sorry, I'm late," he said, and with a huge yawn threw himself down in a chair. "I overslept. We've been having too many late night incidents."

Darren quickly slurped down the energy drink. "I don't think I've had more than eight hours sleep in the last four days. So let's get going. Maybe I'll have time for a nap later," he said with a laugh.

As if that were the cue, phones in the room began beeping as SEV1 alerts came piling in.

After checking his phone, Darren said, "Sorry folks. I've got an incident to deal with, and that takes priority over this. The business comes first, you know. We'll reschedule this for later in the week."

The other members of the problem management meeting nodded in agreement and began following him out.

"Don't go," I said. "Darren may be the problem manager, but I'll fill in for him. We can still have the meeting and fix some of these problems. That will cut down on the alerts. This is very important work."

Nicola stopped long enough to say, "Come to the War Room, Chris. We need your help there. We can't ignore this SEV1. Once it is fixed we can go back to working on problems."

And that was the issue. Problem management would always be a fill-in for whenever there wasn't a SEV1. But the moment there was an alert; problem management would get

7: Time to Refocus

kicked to the side until there was more time. The decision by IT leadership to merge the incident and problem management owners into a single person, just reinforced that approach in the minds of everyone in IT and the business. Problem management could never become effective like that. It was the equal of incident management, and just as important. It deserved the same level of commitment.

I watched in frustration as the meeting attendees filed out behind Darren and headed for the war room. Mia was the last to go.

Just before she walked out the door, Panav, the Unix platform manager, turned and said to me, "I know this is very important work to you, Chris. When I have work conflicts, I always have to ask myself, which work is more important to my customers and users. I've found that the best choice is always the one that brings me more in alignment with my users. I tell my team to listen to the wisdom of our users; the business. I tell my team that if they are not directly serving our users, or serving those employees that serve the users, then they should think long and hard about what they are working on, and why they are doing it. We do not have an excess of resources and any time they are not serving one of those two groups, then they are at risk listening to what they want, rather than what our users want."

As I watched her leave, I thought about what she had said, what Ramesh had done, and what Sean had said. It would be very easy to follow their lead and let problem management go; to make it an auxiliary subset of incident management; to make it an afterthought that was only engaged if there was spare time. There would never be

7: Time to Refocus

enough spare time to mature it to the point where it would be useful.

The number of incidents wasn't down, but the business was happier than it had been before and that seemed to be what mattered most to the company. But I knew we could do better. I decided that the only reason the business and IT leadership wasn't insisting on more, was that they didn't know any better. They had measured success this way for so long they couldn't conceive of any other way.

My job was clear. I had to convince them there was a better way. The question was, could I do it without getting fired?

7: Time to Refocus

Tips that would have helped Chris

Sometimes the solution path you choose comes to a dead-end. It doesn't work. Although you must not be afraid to work through difficult situations, you must also be objective enough to see when something will not work, and courageous enough to retool your solution plan.

You will probably not have a choice of who is part of the solution team. Everyone is motivated by different things. Get to know these people one on one. Understand where your common ground is, and what interests them about the solution. Part of success when leading via influence comes from creating excitement about the work. You are the coach and your role is to creatively blend the best of each team member for group success.

CHAPTER 8: THE FIVE QUESTIONS

I slid the chair closer to Mia's desk and sat down. She was a peer to my manager, Ramesh. Neither of us spoke for a moment. No sweat. I'd learned a long time ago that putting a moment of silence before beginning an important conversation tended to focus everyone on the issue at hand.

Mia was the leader of the DBAs. She'd had this role for the last three years. In that time, she'd successfully turned a chaotic, fractious and generally dysfunctional group of individuals into a highly productive and well-run team. At the same time, her employee survey results showed consistent high marks from her staff for her leadership ... both the ones she hired and the ones she inherited. In fact, her team had the lowest turnover of any in IT. Mia worked hard to continually improve her team and it showed. She was a great manager who cared about her employees, while also keeping her eye on the corporate goals.

Despite her natural skills, and much to the bewilderment of her manager, she showed zero interest in taking on new or larger leadership roles. I'd been told that every time they offered her promotion to a bigger role she turned it down, saying that, "This work is what I am best suited for. Perhaps there is someone else more deserving of these other opportunities."

Mia wasn't her real name. It was one she used at work, rather than having to continually help people pronounce and spell her full name properly, much less explain how Chinese names were presented differently from European names.

8: The Five Questions

Mia addressed the name issue in a way that was practical and pragmatic. I liked that. She did what it took to align with her customers and peers, rather than insisting they adapt to her. I actually kind of admired her for it, because I wasn't sure I could be as flexible about something so personal as my name.

I'd heard she was brilliant and had several advanced degrees in areas of mathematics and computer science that made me panic just thinking about trying to understand them. But unlike the offices' of some other leaders, there were no diplomas, no certificates of achievement, training, or any other indication of work or professional accomplishments in her office. In fact, most of what decorated her cube were a few pictures of family and friends, with a sprinkling of bold and brightly colored drawings by her young children, Ying and Wei.

A person's office tells you a lot about them, sometimes more than they realize. A person's office space is much more than a place where they work. It is also as close to a sanctuary and restorative space as they have at work. Things they choose to surround themselves with are often a reflection of their happy place; a reminder of what gives them pleasure and provides reasons for living. Examining a person's office space also tells you something about what motivates them at work. It has reminders for them of the reasons they are there. When trying to encourage a person to work with me, it always helps to understand what is meaningful to them.

Mia sat there smiling wordlessly, apparently waiting for me, so I spoke first.

"My name is Chris. I don't know if you've heard anything specific about what we're doing. I'm working on a project

8: The Five Questions

to reduce the number of incidents disrupting the work we all do supporting our business partners."

She carefully wrote in a notebook with her pen. After finishing, she sat silently for a few moments, as if contemplating my question, before asking, "That is an important and valuable undertaking that will benefit us all. You must be very proud of having been entrusted with such an assignment."

Funny, I had never considered being tossed in front of the same bus that ran over Sarah to be a source of pride or reflection on the level of trust and confidence leadership had in me. I'd always thought of it as a punishment, and that was the feedback I'd gotten from Sean and others around me. Mia's perspective was different. I guess she was assuming positive intent on the part of leadership, where I had automatically assumed a completely defensive posture. It was an interesting way to think about the assignment. Actually, her perspective was very liberating. I was beginning to like the idea of viewing the assignment as a reward, instead of a punishment.

"Yes, I am," I said. "However, I cannot do it all by myself. I need help from your team."

Mia seemed a little taken aback. "Are you concerned about my team? They have been working very hard to resolve any problems as soon as they are identified. I can show you ... "

I stopped her in mid-sentence, which made her shift nervously in her chair.

"Well, what you said is a good example of one of the things we're trying to do; to get people to use consistent terminology in IT. You talked about resolving problems,

8: The Five Questions

when what I think you were talking about, were what best practice would call incidents."

Mia paused for a moment, and then asked, "Do not incidents generate problems for the business? I know my team treats them that way. That is why ... "

I cut her off in mid-sentence again. This time she pushed her chair back from the desk a little, increasing the distance between us, as I went through an overview of the way ITIL differentiates between incidents and problems, as well as how problem management works.

Mia sat patiently, nodded in all the right places and when I finished, she waited for a few seconds before saying, "Thank you for correcting me. I understand. I will help my team learn the correct way to talk about these events. I will instruct them ... "

"That's great," I interrupted. "I'd be happy to train your team on the ITIL fundamentals. But what I really need their help on is our root cause and remediation activities in problem management."

Mia stared at me for a moment, before saying, "My team currently participates actively in the incident root cause and service restoration activities. How is this different from that effort, or is this just a duplication of efforts? My team works very hard, and does not have an excess of resources to ... "

I jumped in before she finished. "Yes, I know they work hard to restore service, but what you're calling root cause in incident management, is just the incident trigger. We want to make sure we get the true root cause in problem management. And that's where I need some help from you, beyond what your team does for incident management.

8: The Five Questions

Problem management will be meeting once a week and I need you to provide us with help understanding the difference between the incident trigger and the real root cause. And we need you to be able to make commitments on when you will remedy any root causes attributable to you."

Mai closed her notebook and put her pen away. She said, "Thank you for offering us the opportunity to be part of your project. Our team will discuss it at our next meeting, and I will see what we can do."

"That's great," I said. "Thanks for supporting this. I'll send you an invitation to the problem management meetings."

I stood up and headed out of her cube, then stopped and said back over my shoulder, "Oh, and let me know when you want me to come and enlighten your team on what ITIL is all about."

As I headed down the hall, I was really proud of myself. That couldn't have gone any better.

Mia wasn't at the first problem management meeting; or the second or the third. In fact, she never showed up. Neither did anyone from her team.

Every time I reached out to Mia to understand why she wasn't there, I got the same response from her, telling me that they were grateful for the chance to participate and that she would see what she could do. I couldn't figure it out. I was only doing a little better with the other people I needed at the meeting.

I'd intentionally structured the problem management meetings to be composed of managers for each of the technical teams. It was important that the attendees be

8: The Five Questions

people who could make commitments. Since they rarely knew all the deep technical details, they always brought some back-up with them. It got to the point where there were over 20 people in the meeting. And each of them had an opinion.

To make matters worse, the problem management meetings were running long ... very long. So long, in fact, that we weren't even getting to half the events which were candidates for problem management. We'd start reviewing an incident, and before long the entire group would drop into solution mode, each person adding their own perspective on what was wrong and how it should be fixed ... even if they had little to do with it.

I usually let the group run with it, because they eventually came up with the true root cause and a good remediation plan. Sometimes quality takes time, I guess. It just took so long to get there, because everyone wanted to have their opinion heard, even if they didn't have a lot to do with the incident, or the remediation. That was one thing about that group; right or wrong, they were never shy about expressing their opinions. It meant that I had to spend most of my time managing the process in the meeting, to ensure things kept moving forward, rather than being part of the content, and helping them come up with the solution.

The worst part was the finger pointing. It didn't matter which team was involved. As soon as the group sensed that one team or another was responsible for the outage, they all began to pile on, enumerating the faults they perceived in that team – real or imaginary – this incident or another. It didn't take long before everyone adopted a totally defensive attitude; refusing to admit, or even allow the suggestion that their team had in some way been involved in the loss of

8: The Five Questions

service to the business. Since no one would ever admit responsibility, reaching root cause, or identifying remediation, became more and more difficult each meeting.

The log jam of unreviewed SEV1s, unidentified remediation plans, and gaps in our known errors and workarounds database, were becoming intolerable. Incidents were going months without being reviewed by problem management. The tipping point came near the end of the second month of problem management. I'd decided the only way to reduce the backlog was to go to twice a week meetings. Two 90 minute meetings each week was a lot to ask of technical managers, but once they understood why, and saw how much of the backlog we cleaned up, I had been confident they would work even harder. Surely they all understood how important this was.

When the second meeting in that week came around, I was the first one into the conference room. I opened up the conference bridge on the speakerphone, and arranged the working materials around the table so that we would be ready to go on time. I always tried to get there early to make sure no one would show up, and then assume the meeting had been cancelled at the last minute because the room was empty and leave.

It was 10 minutes after the scheduled start time, I was still the only one in the room and the conference bridge was still empty. I started dialling the attendees' cell phones to see where everyone was, but got only voicemail. I dutifully left messages.

After 20 minutes I realized no one was going to show. It wasn't a day where there were other competing special events, or pending holidays. People seemed to have just decided not to participate in the process anymore. I

8: The Five Questions

gathered up the documents, shut off the lights, and closed the door behind me. As I walked back towards my cube, I realized I'd need to try something different if I was to succeed. I was smart enough, and experienced enough, to know that if something isn't working, then you need to acknowledge that and use an alternative. As Einstein reportedly once said, "Insanity is doing the same thing over and over again and expecting different results."

I needed to reach back out to the managers of each of the technical teams ... to let them know I was holding them accountable for their participation, and that they were not meeting expectations. I'd given them a lot of authority to determine what was wrong and how to fix it, but that also meant they were accountable for participating in the process and solutions.

I decided to start with Jose, the leader of the Network team. He was brilliant and highly respected by his peers. His team was involved in some fashion, even if it was just service restoration, in almost every incident we encountered. If I could get him back on track, surely the others would follow.

Jose had initially shown up, but by the fourth meeting he never returned. I'd had a terrible time tracking him down, and could never get a meeting appointment to stick. But I knew he went to the fitness centre a lot, so I started hanging out there as much as possible. Eventually, I saw him come in one day after work and head for one of the treadmills.

I reached him before he could turn it on. "Jose ... Hi, it's me, Chris ... from problem management."

Jose stared at me for a moment, then said, "Oh, yeah. Hi. You work out here, too?"

8: The Five Questions

"Yeah, sure. But right now I want to talk with you for a moment."

Jose started programming his routine into the treadmill.

"Okay, what do you want?"

"We miss you at the problem management meetings. You are an important player in this work. I know you are busy, but we really need your insight if we're going to reduce the number of service disruptions. We try to respect your valuable time, but you are key to our collective success. The better we get at this, the less time it will take each week."

Jose turned on the treadmill and stood on the edge as it came up to speed. "Look, right now you are asking for almost three hours of my time a week. Are you out of your freakin' mind? Even my boss doesn't get three hours of my time a week. If I gave that much time to everyone, nothing would ever get done."

"But this is important to our business partners ... very important. Don't you feel any obligation to them?"

"Yeah, I feel the obligation to actually work on things for them, not have endless dialogues with people who don't know what they are talking about, on areas they have no involvement in." He stepped off the edge of the treadmill and walked straight up to me. He reached out and poked a finger at me. "Frankly, your problem management meetings are a waste of time. And if you think I'm wrong, name one single thing that group has come up with and fixed, that improved what we do for the business?"

I stood silent for a moment. He was right. That was the one thing you could always count on from Jose. He had no

8: The Five Questions

filters when it came to telling you how he felt. You always got the same observational honesty you got from a child. No niceties. No careful phrasing. Just the plain truth as he saw it.

"Look, Jose, if we don't put the time in on these, we can't solve them, and if we can't solve them, then they will reoccur. And that means you and your team will end up spending more and more time chasing down the same issues, over and over. Nothing worth doing is ever easy. It's just like working out and staying in shape."

He walked back over to the treadmill and stepped on, easily matching the fast pace he'd set. "You don't get it, Chris," he said, in words breathy from the exertion. "If you can't figure out a way to actually respect my time, I won't be back, and I know my manager will support me in that. I'll give you one meeting a week, with time not to exceed one hour. Period. Figure out how to make it happen with that level of commitment, or you're doing it wrong. You'll get the same message from everyone else if they've got the *tener cojones* for it."

I walked over and stood directly in front of the treadmill. "If we live with that amount of time, then all we'll have time for in the meeting is just a readout of status by each of the teams. We won't have time to finalize the root cause, or determine the best remediation plan."

The treadmill began to ramp up, and Jose was breathing harder, and sweat was beading on his forehead. "And what's wrong with that? Who says you have to solve the world's problems in one meeting? Quit trying to boil the ocean, and hold teams accountable for working out who owns the event for root cause purposes among themselves. Let them figure out the best remediation plan, and then

8: The Five Questions

have them present it back to a small problem management board, for approval only. Restrict the size of the meeting, and make those attending act like the leaders they get paid to be."

It snapped into place at that moment. Jose was right. I'd been foolish and very disrespectful of the attendee's time. The problem management board was the right way to go. We could use the team owning the incident trigger as the starting owner of the root cause, until they found someone better. But the key was that the technical teams would work that out among themselves. They were used to working together to develop solutions. This would be no different. Besides, while the owner of the root cause usually had some remediation work to do, there were often multiple remediation activities, and usually at least one of them was owned by the team owning the incident trigger.

"Thanks, Jose. You're right. If I promise to make those changes, will you start attending again?"

"If you leave me alone and let me finish my workout, I will give you one more chance. But if you start wasting my time again, I am gone. Do you hear me?"

"Got it. I'll set up the next meeting for two weeks from now."

"Yeah, whatever," said Jose, as he turned up the music on his headset.

As I walked to the door, I made a note to sit down with each of the technical teams as soon as possible, to get them working on the incident triggers they currently owned and let them know what was going to change.

8: The Five Questions

By the time I reached the parking lot, I had it all laid out in my head. Now if I could only figure out why Mia was ignoring me, things would be going great.

Tips that would have helped Chris

IT is one of the most multicultural organizations in the company. Be very aware of cultural sensitivity and body language. People communicate with their words, as well as their voluntary and involuntary body language. Try not to miss any information being given to you. There are many excellent books available on working cross-culturally. Educate yourself and research your contacts before you meet them.

Try to remember that people have additional responsibilities beyond the ones involved in your process. Be sensitive and realistic in the time commitments you ask of them. Use meetings as status events, not as working sessions. Let the SMEs conduct their working sessions outside the meetings. That will keep meetings short and to the point.

CHAPTER 9: WHAT IS THAT LIGHT AT THE END OF THE TUNNEL?

I chugged the energy drink, tossing the empty into the trash and grabbing another in one continuous motion. I held the fresh can's cold surface against my forehead, letting the cool drops of condensation trickle down my face, as I yawned. It felt good. But I was still foggy from the lack of sleep. I'd been working all day, and most of the night, for the last two weeks, and it was catching up with me. Nothing seemed to work to keep me awake anymore.

I was in my spare bedroom; the place I euphemistically called my home office. At least that was the idea I once tried to sell to the tax man ... unsuccessfully, I might add. The clock on my desk added a cool glow to the darkened room. It was nearly 2 am, and my laptop's screen was filled with data. I'd never be ready for my meeting with Ramesh in the morning, but it was my own fault.

I'd been able to build a database containing every incident for the last two years, and by attending every Sev1 response meeting, I was able to collect and add data on the new ones as they occurred. I'd spent the last day and a half going through each of the incidents individually, trying to figure out a way to improve our handling of incidents, so they would simply go away.

I couldn't call what I had information. It would take me all night, and most of tomorrow, just to go through the rest of the detail. I'd been trying to summarize it for hours, but no matter what I tried, it failed. I'd charted and created tables, and means and distributions, but the more I tried, the worse it got.

9: What is that Light at the End of the Tunnel?

There was still too much data. Sure, we'd been able to nail one of those repeating incidents and everyone was happy about that. But if I had to do that for all of them, and every time there was an incident, I would never make it. I was going to need three or four more people just to stay even.

I needed some feedback on that idea before proposing it to Ramesh, so I sent a text to Sean, asking if he'd meet for breakfast in the morning. I hoped he'd see it in the morning and respond, so I was surprised when I got a response from him almost immediately asking, "When and where?"

I had just chugged the energy drink and was washing the taste out of my mouth with a big swig of black coffee, when Sean walked into the restaurant and over to my table. He sat down and shook his head.

"You keep doing that, and you'll rot your stomach, or have a stroke. Maybe both at the same time."

"More job opportunities for you."

Sean laughed as the waitress walked up.

"Morning, Hun," she said. "You want a breakfast, lunch or dinner menu?"

Sean stared at her with a puzzled look. "Do you serve dinner at 6 am?"

She tapped her pad with the eraser end of her pencil. "Look, Hun, we have cops, fire-fighters, third shifters, truckers and computer geeks in here all the time. Who knows what time their internal clock is set for? We serve anything, anytime. And I always offer the choice to those who look the part."

"And so who do we look like," I asked with a grin.

9: What is that Light at the End of the Tunnel?

"I tell you what, Doll. You go and look up 'computer geek' in the dictionary and I'll bet they have your picture there staring back at you."

Sean laughed and said, "Breakfast for both, please."

"None for me," I countered. "I'm good with coffee for now."

"Aren't you eating?" Sean asked.

"I'm afraid it will make me sleepy. I'll get something later."

Sean poured two creams and four sugars into his coffee. "So what was so important you needed to meet before work today?"

"You know that I was able to identify some repeating incidents all caused by the same thing, right?"

Sean nodded as he stirred his coffee, then took a sip. "That was a great piece of work. You should be really proud of that. Don't know how we all missed the connection, but I'm glad you had the insight to spot it."

"Do you know how many incidents I had to read and understand to do that … over 400. It took me weeks to find that one repeater. I've been going through the data looking for others, and everything is all jumbled up in my head now. I can't keep them straight. There's just too much for one person to handle. I could never keep up going forward. I can't even get through all the ones we have. If we are going to do this, it will take more than one person … probably three or four. Either that, or else I'm going to need to call meetings with the technical teams a couple of times a week, so they can explain their notes."

9: What is that Light at the End of the Tunnel?

Sean shook his head. "You're kidding, aren't you? We have a hiring freeze on right now. You may have Jessica's attention at the moment, but your boss will never agree to it. Neither will Jessica. Think it through. If you get a bunch of heads, everyone else will go crazy demanding their own, too ... and for projects that can show a much more concrete ROI that what you're doing. And don't even think about going back to calling a couple of meetings a week about this stuff. Even I won't attend. You're delusional from too little sleep."

"Okay, so what should I do?"

Sean shrugged. "If I knew, then I'd be doing it. But then again I wasn't stupid enough to volunteer for the job without first knowing how I was going to get it done ... like some people."

I drained the last of the coffee in my cup. "You know that I was assigned this task because Sarah failed. Maybe you're next in line for the job if I fail. So if you don't have an idea of what to do, then you'd better get thinking."

Sean shifted uncomfortably in his chair. "Hmmm, that may be true."

I was a little pleased with myself. Up to this point, I had always let Sean box me into a corner, and by giving him back as well as he gave me for the first time, I was actually able to plant the thought in his mind that he had a stake in solving this, too.

The waitress interrupted us with Sean's breakfast. She pointed at me with her pencil and asked, "So Hun, are you gonna eat something or not?" She offered me the Breakfast menu. "Breakfast is really good here. I recommend protein if you're trying to stay awake."

9: *What is that Light at the End of the Tunnel?*

I flipped the menu open. There were at least six pages of breakfast items. There must have been 100 different items. There was every kind of meat I had ever heard of, everything from buffalo sausages to turkey omelettes. There were eggs done more ways that I imagined possible, and the list of pancakes, waffles and crepes seemed to go on forever. It was overwhelming.

"I can't possibly decide," I mumbled. The lack of sleep was fogging my brain. "There are too many to go through. It will take me forever. Why do they make it so complicated?"

She snatched the menu back from me. "Sure you don't work third shift, Darlin? This ain't complicated at all. It only takes a minute to pick something out. Let me show you how. First, do you want Breakfast, Lunch or Dinner?"

""Uh, Breakfast I guess."

"Okay, then you want the breakfast menu." She handed the menu back. "Now, do you want mostly protein, carbohydrate, or sweet? Lookin' at you, I'd head to the protein."

"Okay, protein I guess."

"Are you vegetarian?"

"Nope. I eat pretty much all types of things."

"Low cholesterol or not?"

"Mine is already low. Lucky genes I guess."

"Something exotic, or plain old comfort food?"

"Nothing fancy. Comfort would be good."

9: *What is that Light at the End of the Tunnel?*

The waitress fanned the menu open and shoved it into my hands. "You want something from this section, Hun."

There were eight items in the section titled, "Classic Comfort Breakfasts". Each was a breakfast staple and all met the requirements I had given her. I pointed to the bacon scrambler with smoked Gouda. "I'd like this, but I think I should have something sweet at the end."

Without looking up from her writing, she said, "No sweat, Darlin', just flip to the section called Classic Sweet Endings. It should be two pages further in."

She was right, and it had six items. I chose the chocolate croissant.

The waitress smiled and said, "I'll be back in a few with your food, Darlin."

As she was walking away, Sean started to laugh.

"What's so funny," I asked, afraid he was laughing at me because I had so much trouble ordering breakfast that the waitress had to help. "There were hundreds of things there. It would have taken me forever to go through them all. And then deciding which one I wanted would have been impossible. There were too many things to handle."

Sean shook his head. "You're too close to it. You don't see that she just showed you how to solve your problem about making it easier to uncover repeating outages."

"I order breakfast for everyone?" I was completely confused and so very tired.

"What did she do to make it easy for you?"

"She asked me some questions about what I wanted. Any idiot can do that."

108

9: *What is that Light at the End of the Tunnel?*

"And what did she do with that information?"

I shrugged my shoulders. I really hated these little games Sean loved to play.

Sean reached out and motioned to a server. "May I please see the Breakfast, Lunch and Dinner menus? I think my friend is rather hungry."

The server returned in a moment with the menus. Sean laid them side by side on the table.

"The first thing she did was ask you what meal you wanted. You said breakfast." Sean set the other menus on a chair beside him. "That reduced the number of items by two-thirds."

Sean opened the menu. "Then she asked you if you wanted something from the protein, carbohydrate or sweet." He pointed to each of these sections inside the menu as he spoke. "You said protein." Sean then folded the pages of the menu so that only the protein offerings were visible. "That reduced the number of items by two-thirds again."

Before Sean spoke again, I saw the vegetarian, low cholesterol sections under protein. Looking a little further down the list, I saw a section called "Classic Comfort," with its eight items, one of which had been my choice.

"Get it?" asked Sean as he fanned through the pages of the menu. "You need to segregate the incidents into categories and only consider them one category at a time. Then you'll have small enough numbers that you can get your hands around them. Each meal has a number of category attributes to it."

"So we can tell people how many outages were sausage and how many were eggs?"

9: What is that Light at the End of the Tunnel?

"Something like that. You need to come up with categories that make sense for IT. Start with People – Process – Technology. Fit every incident into one of those categories. Then fit every incident into another layer of categories about what was going on when it happened. Use something like, making a routine change, installing something new; things like that. Or maybe even nothing. The incident trigger happened all on its own."

It all snapped into place. It almost made too much sense. "And then I could add the team that either caused, or could have done something to prevent it from happening. It's like a database with each event as an entry. And each of those entries has attribute fields ... one for each category. So I can sort and group the events by category. Based on that, I can identify trends by area of interest and impact."

I started sketching designs and making notes on the napkin, not realizing it was cloth, not paper. "I'll want to get with our Mia and her DBA team to see if they can adapt the ticketing tool to do this. And if not, maybe they can build me a relational database that each of the technology teams can use to enter ... "

Sean cut me off. "Ease off on the caffeine, Chris. You're getting ahead of yourself. This is not the time to boil the ocean. Keep it simple and small. If you can't quickly build a workable tool using a spreadsheet, then you're making it too complicated. Perfection is not required. All you need is some improvement."

Sean took a sip of his coffee and added, "Just be cautious about pointing fingers, because you'll drive people away. It's about all of us getting better through continual improvement, not about achieving instant satori."

9: *What is that Light at the End of the Tunnel?*

I nodded. It all slipped into place. I just had to figure out which categories made the most sense, and remember that any event has multiple categories. The biggest risk to any work is the fear to step back and get a broader view of what's important and what needs to be done. Being too close to the details, or too invested in the way things were always done, makes continual improvement that much harder.

I was so excited by the breakthrough, that I immediately sent a text to Ramesh telling him I was sick in bed and we'd need to reschedule. I used a text so I wouldn't have to actually speak with him. I couldn't have him finding out where I really was.

"My apologies, Sean, but I'm going home to work on this right now," I said as I stood up and pushed my chair in. "Thank you so much for all your guidance. You really showed me a breakthrough."

I put 20 dollars down on the table. "Here, this should be enough to cover your breakfast and the tip."

Sean started laughing at me. "You are insane … in a good way, I guess. Best of luck. Remember, keep it simple."

I nodded and walked away. I didn't care if he was laughing. Now I had a way to boil the ocean … one category at a time.

9: What is that Light at the End of the Tunnel?

Tips that would have helped Chris

Ideas for solutions will come from the strangest places. Don't be afraid to ask for input, or consider non-IT solutions that could be adapted to your situation. Elements of the ITSM process can be seen in other businesses, and other industries. Don't discount inspiration because of its source.

Solution inspiration often comes in bursts. It rarely comes a little bit at a time. Try to strike a balance between digging deeper and trying something different. People often confuse effort and results; thinking that working harder and longer on something will produce results, when in fact, they have already gleaned everything they can use from that source and need to move on to another venue.

CHAPTER 10: NOT EVERYONE LIKES ANSWERS

I flipped to the last slide and the words, "The End," filled the screen. I waited a moment and then asked, "Are there any questions?"

Jessica and her staff sat silently around the table, still staring at the screen. The only exception was Ramesh. He was watching Jessica, looking for some hint of her reaction.

I was confident the message from my presentation had been overwhelming. Even Ramesh had been stunned into silence when I showed it to him yesterday. After seeing it, he was more excited about any of my work than I had seen him in a long time. He even ended the meeting by assuring me that together we were going to make this happen. It felt really good to have him backing me.

My root cause analysis showed statistically how 83% of our incidents were due to the activities of people; that 78% of our preventable incidents were due to approved change activity; that 43% of our incidents were repeats, nearly identical to previous incidents; and that collectively, the DBA, UNIX and software development teams were responsible for 87% of our incidents. These four dimensions were the low-hanging fruit just waiting to be plucked. Making an improvement in these areas would have a leveraged effect on reducing the number of incidents impacting our business partners.

I was proud ... really proud of what I had done. And not just because all of the data on incidents had been reduced to a few core bits of actionable information. I had also crystallized a methodology for categorization and filtering

10: Not Everyone likes Answers

that we could use going forward. I had just presented the IT leadership with a way to make problem management a practical tool to reduce the number of incidents. And that was the issue that had ended more than one person's career here. But I had beaten it. Today was my day to be the hero.

After a moment of silence, Clement, the VP of software development, closed his notebook and pushed back from the table. He crossed his arms and said, "I don't believe it."

Clement was not new to his role, or the company. He'd been software development VP for the last six years and with the company for over 20 years. He'd worked his way up in the company from third shift computer operator, to his current position. Rumour was that he had no aspirations for any further roles at the company; that he was quite happy where he was and wanted to stay there.

Everyone in the room turned to Clement. "Each element of our development activity is rigorously tested and corrected during development, and before we release it into the environment, so I know my team's work cannot be the source of these incidents. Clearly, there is an error in the data, or the analysis. Obviously, Chris has expended a lot of effort here, and I am sure we all are appreciative of his attempt to reign in what continues to be a chronic irritation for everyone. Personally, I've seen Chris here working at all hours of the day and night. I don't know of anyone who's worked harder at trying to fix our situation."

Clement gestured to me with a cloying smile. "Thank you Chris, for your commitment and industriousness."

He looked at the rest of Jessica's directs sitting around the table, and continued in a more solemn tone. "But effort alone doesn't make it correct. Perhaps due to Chris'

10: Not Everyone likes Answers

inexperience or unfamiliarity with what my team does, many of these incidents have been inaccurately categorized. Everyone knows that categorization is difficult to use and can produce misleading results. In development, we study human factors, and we know that when presented with lists of categories, people tend to pick only from the first few. So I suspect the data may be skewed, due to what we call selection order effects. That's where, when presented with a long lists of choices, people gravitate towards the first few, even though better choices may exist further down the list."

Clement gestured to Ramesh. "If you'd like, I can have one of my experts educate Chris, explaining this effect in detail, and perhaps providing some guidance on better ways for Chris to approach the analysis, so it is more accurate and more in line with how people think and act. We have a great deal of experience in these matters on my team."

I waited for Ramesh to defend me. He had been so certain and supportive last night. But he just sat there and looked to Jessica. Jessica didn't respond to Clement, or even seem to react to him.

Jessica gestured to Ross, the VP of infrastructure. Ross had emigrated from Edinburgh eight years ago and was incredibly smart. When I had a chance to speak with him, I was struck by how modest and self-effacing he was. He never beat you with his brain power. He always gave you the chance to uncover some insight he knew, but also understood that you would only appreciate if you discovered yourself. I hoped to work with him some day.

Jessica asked, "Ross, what is your reaction to Chris' presentation? Do you think there is some truth in what he is saying?"

10: Not Everyone likes Answers

Ross pondered for a moment, "I know that my teams get paged out a lot during incidents and are key players in their timely resolution. The constant disruption of their lives is one of the major complaints I hear from them. I am willing to look at any approach that can improve the delivery of services to our business partners and help our employees maintain a good work–life balance. Based on the information Chris presented, I'm disappointed with my organization's performance and accept responsibility for changing our behavior ... especially if that improves the relationship with our business partners, and gives my team more of their lives back."

Clement leaned toward Jessica and said, "I think that whatever we do, or don't do, should be consistent across all of IT. While no one will agree that our current situation is ideal, for each of us to act, or not act in our own way on the data Chris has presented, would only make things worse. I feel very strongly that we need to act consistently. We need to act as a unified team. Otherwise our business partners will lose even more faith in us."

Jessica nodded and mumbled murmurs of agreement filled the room.

Jessica sat silently for a moment, biting her lower lip.

She turned to me and said, "Chris, you have done a fantastic job providing all of this information to us. You've helped reduce the number of incidents, and given us insight as to what our next steps need to be for the enablement of effective problem management. But that said, I think we need to pause for a while and assess the impact of what you are asking the organization to do in six months. There are a lot of demands being placed on the organization, and more are coming. We don't want to make too many changes all at

10: Not Everyone likes Answers

once and destabilize the entire organization. But please don't take this as a rebuke or rejection of the information you've provided. I appreciate, and I know the rest of my team appreciates, that you've done."

She turned to Ramesh and asked, "What do you think? As the direct leader of Chris, the person who has had the most exposure to this, what do you think? Do you agree with the idea of giving the organization a chance to absorb all the changes so far, before we give them more?"

Ramesh smiled and in a loud firm voice said, "I couldn't have said it better, Jessica. Chris has done a great job so far, and by holding off for six months on further changes to our processes, there will be time to gather more information, and confirm the accuracy of both the data and the methodology."

He nodded to Clement. "And, of course, we will take you up on your generous offer to assist us." Looking at the rest of Jessica's direct reports, he added, "And we welcome any feedback, or support, any of you cares to provide, so that we can do a better job serving your teams and our business partners."

I tried hard not to show a reaction. I should have known that Ramesh would bend whichever way Jessica went. His corporate survival skills were too finely honed to do otherwise.

Our presentation over, Ramesh and I left the meeting. As I closed the door behind us, he put his hand on my shoulder, smiled and said, "You did a great job. Don't worry about the six-month delay. That's just high-level IT leadership politics. Keep refining your problem management process, and before you know it, we'll be implementing it."

10: Not Everyone likes Answers

Before I could say anything, his phone rang. "I've got to take this," he said, and wandered away chatting on the phone.

I worked my way over to Meredith's cube. Meredith had become the closest thing the business had to a single point of contact for IT. She'd been a product manager for a number of years and under her direction some great new products had been rolled out. She'd been out under maternity leave for 12 weeks early last year for the birth of her daughter. While she was out, her group brought in a new leader and reorganized. That new leader brought in a number of new product managers from their old firm and let some of the legacy employees go. While Meredith had been welcomed back and given a job at the same grade as the one she had previously, none of her projects seemed to have quite the same high visibility as before. Those projects all seemed to go to the people recently hired by the new leader. But she seemed determined to not let herself become a victim. She stepped up at every opportunity to impress her leadership and convince them she was ready for some more important work.

That's why I liked working with her. I'd worked with Meredith on the incident management process, and she had been fairly supportive. At least as much as one could expect when you were asking them to sell their organization on material changes to the way they were doing things. She was more than willing to get her hands dirty on new work, especially if she felt it would get a positive response from her leadership. Meredith didn't always agree with what I thought or wanted to do, but there were plenty of opportunities for things that would benefit us both.

10: Not Everyone likes Answers

She was in her cube as I stepped in and sat down across the desk from her.

"So I heard you got the brush-off from your leadership. That must have felt good," she said.

"How did you know," I asked. "We just finished an hour ago."

Meredith shook her head. "There are no secrets here. Information is power, and the people that have it are not shy about wielding it."

"You mean Jessica passed the word along?" I couldn't believe she would humiliate me like that.

"No, I'm talking about the holders of real power in the company. The people who know everything about everyone, and have the ear of every decision maker ... the administrative assistants. They share the word among themselves."

I laughed. "So if I want to know what's really going on, I should count on the admins to give me the straight answer?"

"No better or faster source out there. They don't have a lot of rank on the org chart, but because of the access they have, and the information they control, they are definitely players behind the scenes. That's why you always want to be their friend. And never ever forget administrative professional's day. Get them some flowers, take them to lunch, or do something that will be meaningful for them, so they will not forget you. Trust me, it's well invested."

I nodded. "Thanks for the advice. What do you think about categorization of incidents, so we can focus on the events that matter?"

10: Not Everyone likes Answers

"I think you messed it up big time. When you call out a senior leader in front of their boss for being a primary contributor to service disruptions, you are asking to get shut down. Especially if they don't know you are going to do it beforehand."

"But I told them it was about all of us working together to make things better. I didn't even try to point fingers."

"Doesn't matter what your intentions are. It matters how your actions are perceived."

"But Jessica ... and even my own boss, should have stood up and helped me. They could have added clarification, and helped those leaders feel better about it."

"Don't be naive, Chris. Ramesh has outlived three CIOs, and will probably outlive Jessica, at the rate I hear she's been going. He's going to take all his cues from the others in that room. He'll stand up for you, but only if he feels it won't hurt him. It's not that he doesn't like you, or support you. It's just that his survival comes first. He'd probably weasel it around so it sounds like he is looking out for your best interests, but take it from me, Ramesh is only concerned about himself."

"But what about Jessica? She's the one who gave me the assignment. Why wouldn't she support me?"

"Public flogging for disobeying or refusing orders is allowed here. Leaders here only get to stay around if their team is willing to work for them. Authority is what you give people. If you don't submit to their authority, then they don't have much. Sure, a leader can always fire everyone who doesn't support them. But after the first couple, their leader is going to figure out something is wrong with them and want to get them out. You can kick one or two people

10: Not Everyone likes Answers

out, but if you try to get rid of most of your department, then the powers that be will usually get rid of you instead. It's a lot easier to replace one leader than it is to replace an entire department."

"So what does that have to do with Jessica?" I asked.

"She couldn't very well force half her team to do something they refused to do, even under threat of termination. Threats are a crummy way to lead, and will never work for long, because eventually she'd have to follow through and start firing some of her directs. And those folks have all been here a long time. They are well connected. They wouldn't go easily, and definitely not without letting their network in the company know what a lousy leader Jessica has become. See ... it really doesn't matter what level of leader you talk about. They are all subject to the same rules of retention and coercion."

"You are really cynical and bitter," I said.

"Nope, just a realist. You will be, too, once you've been here long enough. Being realistic about how people work, and act, and think, is the only way you can be effective in getting things done and changing behavior," she said.

"Well that's still discouraging," I said. "Looks like I'm left with no one to support rolling our problem management with categorization."

"Well, you can always get the support of the business. With them behind you, IT would line up in a minute. They know where the money comes from, and if the people providing the money think this is a good idea, then your leadership will, too."

10: Not Everyone likes Answers

I smiled and leaned across the desk. "So Meredith, does that mean you will help me make this happen?"

She laughed and sat back in her chair. "Not on a bet. You don't have a chance, and I need to make sure I'm associated with successes if I'm going to get back into the fast lane. Nothing personal, but the answer is a clear, definite and final, no."

Tips that would have helped Chris

Try to speak individually beforehand with each of the participants at an important presentation. This will tell you what the issues are before the meeting, so you can develop a mitigation strategy. It will also prevent them from being surprised during the meeting. People don't like surprises in business. All it takes is one person with questions and reservations to derail your solution acceptance.

Despite your best efforts, some people may tell you beforehand they will support your solution, but if they sense others are not supporting it, they will change their position simply for their own benefit. While you can't always identify these people in advance, you can at least learn from the experience, and treat their commitments as tentative in the future.

CHAPTER 11: WHY SERVICE OUTAGES ARE LIKE DANDELIONS

The War Room was jammed and noisy. The air was stale, and smelled of carpets and furniture that hadn't been cleaned in a long time. Several large bags of empty Chinese take-out containers were overflowing the trash can. And someone was already making the fourth pot of coffee.

The good news was, we were just starting to get some traction on the first SEV1 service outage of the evening, when the second one cascaded in. But nobody got flustered like in the old days. The incident response team passed the work out, and assigned people to the second one without a hitch.

All the work everyone had put into improving incident management was paying off. The junior SMEs were focused on restoration and workarounds, while the more senior staff dug into the events, trying to identify and capture key bits of data that would prove critical later, during the root cause phase of problem management.

I was really proud of them, and I guess a little of myself. I was the architect behind the new processes. I had translated the standards into procedures and tasks that meshed well with our organization and skill sets. The tools were still crude. We were loading data into spreadsheets and simple databases, but that had been a conscious decision. It didn't make sense to stand up a tool until we knew what we needed that tool to do. I kept reminding myself, first people, then process, then tools.

11: Why Service Outages are like Dandelions

It had taken a lot of work to get incident management aligned with problem management, so both processes were using the same categorization schemes. I'd long since lost track of how many hours I'd spent with each of the technical teams convincing them to give it a chance. Fortunately, it had paid off almost immediately.

Now it was so much easier to track incidents directly, from incident management, through root cause and remediation. Trends were even starting to appear. The problem management meetings were now reasonably well attended by the managers of the technical teams, and although it took us a little while, everyone was finally in sync, that the meeting was not a working session; that it was strictly a status readout and making commitments. I knew that Ramesh was pleased at how far we'd come when he started asking when problem management was going to start reducing the number of incidents. And in talking with one of Mia's DBAs, I discovered what a cultural klutz I had been during my meeting with her. It had taken a little while, but I had even repaired that relationship, and she was now participating in problem management, along with everyone else.

But two major SEV1s at the same time was going to be a challenge. It would mean careful prioritization of resources. Sean was a great help there. He seemed to instinctively know where and how he could skimp at any given moment, without slowing down the final result. It was almost as if, from experience, he was able to carry a master project plan around in his head.

I was feeling confident we would be able to handle today's issues, when an alert for the third SEV1 popped up on my phone, followed less than two minutes later by a fourth. I

11: Why Service Outages are like Dandelions

stuck my phone back in my pocket, only to have it start ringing again. I felt only a little better when I saw it was Ramesh, and not another SEV1 coming in.

"Hi Ramesh, what can I do for you?"

"Chris, what is the status of the incidents? We seem to be having a lot of them all at once. Why is that?" From the echo in his voice, he was on speakerphone. I waited for a second to see if he would let me know who was there with him. It wasn't forthcoming. I tried to be subtle.

"I'm here in the War Room. We're working on it right now. We'll get all services restored as quickly as possible. Does anyone there with you have questions?" Not an overly slick way for him to tell me who else was with him, but about as direct as I thought I could be.

"This is Jason, the VP of sales and marketing, and I want to know what the hell is going on," boomed a resonant voice. Jason had a reputation as the golden rainmaker as far as the business was concerned. No matter what the economic situation, product status, or customer issue, his team always came back with the sale and made the revenue. From what I'd read in the annual report, he was very well compensated for his efforts. More importantly, since his team was the one that delivered the company's revenue, he pretty much got whatever he wanted, whenever he wanted it.

"We're executing our incident management process," I said. "We're focused on getting these IT services restored to you as quickly as possible. We have representatives from each of the technical teams, as well as our known error and workaround database. We'll be … "

Jason cut me off. "Don't ever tell me what you are going to do, because I don't work on promises. I want commitments

11: Why Service Outages are like Dandelions

to solutions and closure. I want to know why we're continuing to have these disruptions in service, and when they will stop. I was promised you were going to make these disruptions go away. You seem to be failing from where I sit."

"I apologize for the disruption of IT services, Jason. While the incident is not my fault, I do accept it as my problem to investigate and identify some preventative remediation."

"Being willing to fall on your sword does not impress me," snapped Jason. "Frankly, I don't care if you keep your job or not. All I care about is stopping IT from continually disrupting the hard work of my team due to IT's inability to do anything without breaking it."

I wasn't going to rise to the verbal bait and get in an argument with Jason. That seemed to be what he wanted. I simply reminded myself that this wasn't personal; it wasn't about me.

"We'll be assessing today's events during the problem management meeting tomorrow," I said. "If you, or any of your team, would like to attend, we would love the participation."

"If I send one of my staff to your meeting," said Jason. "Will you waste their time, or will you actually fix the source of these disruptions?"

"There is more value we add to it."

"Here it comes," said Jason. There was a moment of silence, then I heard him in a much quieter voice say, "Yes ... it's on mute, Ramesh. Don't worry. They can't hear us. Do you have a replacement available for Chris? Every word I hear sounds like a loser forecasting more failure coming

11: Why Service Outages are like Dandelions

down the road at us. Chris should go sooner rather than later. I don't know what you are waiting for. Just pull the damn trigger, man."

"Don't worry," said Ramesh. "Succession planning is a key part of what I do for all of my employees. I have someone lined up and ready."

"You've talked to them about it?" asked Jason.

"Absolutely," said Ramesh. "They understand the full situation, and are eager to step in if Chris can't fix things."

"Good," said Jason. "But I wouldn't wait too long. Because if things don't improve quickly, or they get worse, I will be having a similar conversation with Jessica about you. Do you understand?"

"Got it," said Ramesh.

There was the beeping of some fumbled buttons on Ramesh's phone and then his voice.

"Sorry we had to drop off, Chris. Jessica stopped by ... "

Jason added, "And she wanted to talk about a few things that didn't involve you."

I smiled because although I had found out weeks ago that the mute button on Ramesh's speakerphone no longer worked, obviously he hadn't figured it out yet.

"No problem," I said. "I don't need to be burdened with things that don't involve me or my work."

The problem management meeting started right on time. Jason had assigned Meredith as his representative at the meeting. I'd worked with her before the meeting, so that she was fully briefed on the problem management process.

11: Why Service Outages are like Dandelions

As usual, the first thing we did was review the incoming SEV1 incidents that had occurred since the last meeting, to determine if they should be taken through the full root cause process of problem management, or simply filed for future reference, either because the risk of recurrence was low, they were part of an existing problem already being worked, they had a very low impact, or because there simply wasn't enough forensic information to make a root cause determination. This was a data filter we used to ensure that we focused on the events that were important, and that we had a chance of impacting.

Of the five SEV1s we'd had in the last week, it turned out that only one was appropriate for problem management. Three of them had insufficient forensic evidence to even attempt a complete root cause. The other one was a complete one-off, and everyone agreed the odds of something like that happening again were minimal.

I had explained this part of the process thoroughly to Meredith, and I thought she understood that some, but not all SEV1s, end up getting a full and final root cause in problem management. Some go no further than the incident trigger stage of analysis. During the briefing, she'd been resistant to a lot of what I'd told her, and occasionally turned almost hostile. But I thought we had reached an agreement as professionals that, while we might personally disagree on some details, we were both working toward the same ends, and could work together using this process for the good of the company. It turns out my assessment of her state of mind was all wrong.

"Everyone needs to stop right now," she said. "This is just not right. We need to be doing a full root cause on every SEV1 that occurs. We can't just toss the hard ones away

11: Why Service Outages are like Dandelions

and concentrate only on the easy ones. Why do you even bother meeting. This is just a waste of time if you throw out these incidents that are hurting the business."

"We don't throw them away," I responded. "They become part of our database that we use when evaluating whether or not new SEV1s should go through root cause. We keep them around just in case patterns start to occur. What we don't do is, take up a lot of time doing root causes that realistically will have little operational or preventative benefit."

"That may be good in theory," added Meredith. "But from what I can see, you haven't really had any success using this plan, have you? The number of incidents remains unchanged, and if last week is any indicator, they have actually increased. How does your theory respond to the fact that incidents are actually increasing, because of the way you run these meetings?"

"We don't run these meetings based on theory," I said. "We take all that we have learned, and continue to learn and continually improve, and upgrade, the process."

"Well then, you must not have learned much, because what you're doing isn't working. In sales and marketing we measure success by results, and so far no one has seen any." She gestured around at the entire room. "You ... all of you, are hurting the business and our customers by what you're doing. I don't care if you waste your own time. IT seems pretty good at that. But when you're fiddling around reduces the company's opportunities for success; then I get mad. So please excuse my being emotional and disrupting the meeting, but this company means a lot to me. Too many people are working too hard to make it a success, for me to sit idly by and watch you do nothing to help it."

11: Why Service Outages are like Dandelions

"Meredith, it's not a question of supporting, or not supporting, the company. It's about leveraging the resources IT has, by first focusing on what matters most. We start there and grow better. That is ... "

"No, Chris," said Nicola. "Meredith is correct. The only measure that matters is whether or not we have succeeded in reducing the number of incidents. Everything else is just about the method of execution."

"He's right," said Jose. "Look at how many incidents we actually took into problem management for root cause and remediation. There aren't that many."

"Did the ones we took in get all the way through and actually get remediated?" I asked.

"Yeah," said Jose.

"And of the ones that were remediated, where things were changed in technology, processes, or people activities; have any of those recurred. Have they become repeats?"

"Well, no."

"And had any of them been recurring issues occurring over and over again that continued to impact the business?"

"No," offered Mia. "My team was very pleased that we addressed the issue of memory leaks on the Windows® servers that kept corrupting the database indexes, and requiring substantial downtime on all the Windows® servers to repair."

"Yes," I offered. "That was a huge event when that happened. Do you remember that, Meredith?"

11: Why Service Outages are like Dandelions

"Yes, that was right after I came back to work from my maternity leave. But there were plenty of other issues at the same time."

"Yes, and that's because by closing off some of the biggest pain points, we can focus on others. Look, things will always break. People will always make mistakes. Incidents will never go away. Problems will always be with us. What's important, is that we continually work on finding them and clearing them out. Problem management is not about getting to a point where there are no incidents. That will never happen. Problem management is about having a rational, cost-effective way to separate lesser issues from those with the potential to seriously damage the company, and then focusing on the subset of those that you can actually fix. Over time the definition of what constitutes a substantial issue may change, and even when you think you have them all handled, more will erupt."

"So what you are saying," said Nicola. "Is that our work here will never reach a destination, it will always be on a journey of improvement, and how we make that journey is the value we add to the company."

I smiled. "Nicola, are you trying to get my job now?"

11: Why Service Outages are like Dandelions

Tips that would have helped Chris

Take a moment now and then to assess how far you have come. It is easy to look only at how far you have to go. Looking at where you began, and where you are now, is very important and energizing. Celebrate your success. You have earned it.

At the end of the day, it does not matter how efficient or ITIL compliant your solution is. What matters is how effective your solution is in reducing pain on your users. It is easy to spot the people who confuse this by looking at the metrics they use to measure their performance. How many of your KPIs and metrics track user experience and satisfaction, versus how many track how well items move through your solution process? If it is mostly the latter, then you should consider some new metrics and a shift in focus.

CHAPTER 12: WHEN NO ONE IS AROUND

I chugged the energy drink, then tossed the empty into the trash, and grabbed another from the break room fridge in one continuous motion. I held the fresh can's cold surface against my forehead, letting the cool drops of condensation trickle down my face as I yawned. My eyes hurt, and I was having trouble focusing on the laptop screen. I knew you weren't supposed to rub your eyes, but I did anyway. They were so dry, it felt like I was grinding sand into them.

It was nearly 2 am. I knew my laptop would be waiting for me back in my cube; its screen still filled with too much data, all waiting for my analysis. I looked at the vending machines to see if there were anything to eat that wouldn't make me sick, but stepped away when I realized I was just trying to avoid going back to work. My back ached as I stretched before walking out into the hall. Here and there, cubicles had lights on, but there was no way of knowing if that was someone still working, or just a lazy attempt to make their manager think they were working late.

I was really beginning to resent the constant struggle to sustain even some level of effective participation by the IT leaders in my problem management process. Every step away by them meant that I had to do that much more. At times I was way beyond driving the root cause of incidents. I was actually trying to help the technicians work through their issues. That was the only way I could get them to participate. They respected the commitment on my part, even if I didn't know that much. Maybe my being there just gave them someone to feel smarter than. But it was still wrong on so many levels.

12: When No One is Around

To get the oxygen flowing in my brain, I took the long way back to my cube. A little exercise was just what my body needed tonight. The walk took me past the data centre.

The data centre had an unusual construction; expensive, too. A non-negotiable request from a previous CIO during the data centre build-out was for transparent walls along one side, so that they could walk guests by and impress the unknowing with all the rows of blinking lights, and the sterile look of the space. Very inefficient from a facility standpoint, but who knew what pressures the CIO was under at the time.

I took this hall many times during the day, and the data centre had always been devoid of people. But that made sense. The business had insisted on a standing rule of no changes during their prime hours of 7 am to 8 pm. And with the new customer relationship management system, Mountain Top, rolling out to the field in two days, they'd insisted on a total freeze, except for emergency repairs. Everyone had been sent a copy. The memo was posted on almost every wall, and even on the doors to the data centre.

I stopped when I noticed people inside the data centre. At first I thought they might be operators loading a tape or something. When I saw three people sliding a server into a rack, pulling floor tiles, and pulling wires up out of the floor for power and connection, I knew something was wrong. I checked my phone, but there was nothing about an outage. I swiped my badge on the door card reader, and to my surprise, the door clicked open. That shouldn't happen. I shouldn't be allowed inside unescorted. As I stepped into the mantrap, I wondered how many other people had unrestricted access.

12: When No One is Around

A moment after the outer door sealed, the inner door opened. I stepped into the data centre, as a rush of cool air pushed up through the floor from the plenum underneath. Now I could hear laughter and voices. They sounded only a couple of rows to my left. I recognized the voices. It was Nidal, Roger and Shelia. They worked on the development team. I'd met all of them one time during an employee after-hour's party. At least they were laughing. It's good to enjoy your work, I guess.

I reached their aisle just as they locked the new server into the uppermost space in the cabinet, and began snapping power and network cables into the back.

"Hey, Chris. Great timing. You show up just as we're finishing up our work. If you'd been here a few minutes earlier, you could have given us a hand to get this server in, so we can get loading the user interface for Mountain Top. You have the timing of a manager, that's for sure." They all laughed and kept working.

I shook my head. "What are you guys doing here? Why aren't the data centre folks racking and stacking for you?"

Shelia giggled, "Cause they're lazy. Getting them to do what it takes to get the job done, is like pushing a string. They don't care a whole lot about meeting the needs of the business. The only time line they work by is their own. They've got so many work rules and schedules, that it's worse than working with a bunch of paper-pushing bureaucrats. They have no concept of the word urgent, and don't seem to care that this application needs to be functional for the business in two days."

"Yeah," interrupted Nidal. "They're a bunch of bureaucrats who never want to step up and go the extra mile when the

12: When No One is Around

situation demands it. And they don't understand what it is they are putting in. They're not the ones who slaved for the last eight months over the code on this server we're installing." He pointed to the three of them. "Look at us. Here we are making sure this gets done, even though we really should be home in bed asleep. But we do this because that's what it takes for the business to be successful. We're the kind of IT people that you can count on to deliver ... the kind that make IT a good business partner with the business. The company needs more people like us ... people of action, and a lot fewer zombies like the ones that work third shift in the data centre."

"You mean this is critical to Mountain Top going live in two days?"

Roger nodded, "Unless of course you'd prefer it not to work. Back-end functionality isn't much good to the average salesperson without some front-end GUI."

I couldn't believe what I was hearing. I'd sat through the change management meeting three weeks ago, where the installation of Mountain Top was reviewed and approved. The leaders from the development team assured us that the application had successfully passed all unit and integrated system testing. They told the change management board that all development work was completed. Even the manager of these three had been there, and assured everyone that the GUI was ready to go.

"But what about the change management meeting a couple of weeks ago?" I said.

Roger shrugged. "Who knows? I wasn't there. I just know we had to get the Mountain Top roll out approval from change management by that date, so we could support the

12: When No One is Around

business. But why the inquisition, Chris? You're the one always talking about how we need to support the needs of the business. We did what we had to do, so that the business can move forward in two days. Isn't that what a good IT business partner does?"

So the input from the change requestors had been all smoke and mirrors. They'd lied their way through the meeting in order to meet the deadline the business had set.

"But how did you get this change approved? Was it okayed as an emergency change?" I asked, afraid that I already knew the answer.

"We don't need a change to install our own servers in an empty rack, right gang?" Nidal and Shelia nodded.

"There's no question it needs to be done ASAP. So that makes approval moot," said Shelia, as she snapped the last cable into the back of the server. "And if we'd asked, there was a chance some bureaucrat on the change board would have found a reason to make us put it off. They're not accountable for keeping the company going. All they have to do is keep their chair warm."

Shelia slapped the side of the rack. "Besides, we've installed servers a hundred times before. Any 12 year old can do it. It's the only server in the rack. There is no risk here. And we're doing it for the right reason ... because the business demands it."

She turned to Nidal and asked, "Shall we fire this puppy up and see if it lives?"

"Hell yeah," said Nidal, as he ran his hand across the power switch. "I validate this code load so I can go home and get my life back."

12: When No One is Around

"But what about integration testing? Did you test this final version with the rest of Mountain Top? What if it impacts the rest of Mountain Top?"

"Don't be such a worrier," said Nidal. With a wide swing of his arm, he slapped the power switch to on, and said with a giggle, "It's alive! It's alive!"

This was very wrong. I started to say, "Stop," but the words never made it out of my mouth.

"We did it," said Nidal, as he leaned up against the server and slapped his hand against the rack really hard. Roger yelled, "Oh, shit … ," as the entire cabinet, server and all, began to tip over directly at me.

In their haste, the trio had grabbed the only empty cabinet they could find. To protect the data centre they must have thought. What they didn't know was that they had grabbed a cabinet that had simply been staged on the floor. It wasn't yet bolted down and with the server incorrectly bolted in at the very top, the entire cabinet was unstable.

The toppling cabinet knocked me backwards and I watched in what seemed to be slow motion as Nidal's hands reached around the rack, trying to keep it from landing on me. Shelia and Roger both grabbed for the sides, but couldn't hold on. My rear hit the raised floor hard, my back slapping into the cabinets in the next row just an instant before Nidal lost his grip and the rack slammed into the cabinet behind me. The cabinet behind my back shook and tilted. Sparks flew as cables were severed, but it remained upright enough to prevent the loose rack from crushing me.

"Are you okay," said Shelia, as she peered at me squeezed between the fallen cabinet and the one behind my back.

12: When No One is Around

"As far as I can tell, other than some bruises, the only thing injured is my dignity."

"Thank God," she replied.

I heard Roger's muffled voice in the background.

"We're going to go ... go and get help," said Shelia, her voice sounding very tentative. "Don't worry; you won't be in there long."

I heard feet running away as Nidal and Roger's voices faded. I tried to extricate myself, but the weight of the cabinet was too much for me to lift from a sitting position.

There was a moment of quiet, broken only by the sound of air flowing up from the plenum beneath me, before strange new voices came near.

"Hey, there's someone trapped under the rack. Come on, give me a hand."

The cabinet began to rise as an unfamiliar woman with dreadlocks, and an ear full of piercings, squatted down beside me. "Are you hurt?" she asked.

I sat there, squeezed between the fallen cabinet and the one behind my back. As near as I could tell, nothing was damaged beyond my dignity. I was just stuck and couldn't get out until someone pulled the rack off me. I shook my head, no.

She smiled a wide, toothy grin. "Well, good. Because Brad himself is going to want to publicly kill you when he finds out what you just did here."

"What happened to Roger and Shelia and Nidal? They were right here?"

12: When No One is Around

"Oh they left. No big deal, they're in here all the time. They bring us coffee and sweets to help us make it through the night. They're great people."

"Well, then who are you?"

"Oh, I'm part of the third shift data centre crew. You know, data centre operations. We do adds, moves, changes ... run some jobs ... things like that. That's why Nidal and his gang are great to have around. On nights like tonight when we are really busy, they're always happy to give us a hand and do theirs themselves. It helps us meet our schedules and keeps Brad happy."

My phone went off with a long cascade of severity one outages. Top on the list was Mountain Top. Within seconds, messages from Ramesh, Jessica and Jason popped up on my phone.

A moment later my phone rang, and without thinking, I answered it. It was Ramesh. I wasn't really surprised. Who else would call me at this hour?

"Chris, where are you?"

"I'm in the data centre."

"What are you doing there? Don't you know there is an outage? Mountain Top has gone down. Why aren't you on your way to the War Room to manage the incident?"

I was please Ramesh got the terminology right; although I had the sense this one would definitely merit examination as a problem.

"I'm just ... sitting here getting some assistance from the data centre crew," I said, peering through the gap between the rack pinning me down and the floor, watching feet gathering around the rack and hands trying to free me.

140

12: When No One is Around

Ramesh got louder and clearly more frustrated. "Well there is nothing the data centre operators can do for you right now. I want you down in the War Room as quickly as possible."

"I don't know about that. Right now, their help is pretty essential. But I'll be there as quick as I can," I said, wondering if there were any way I could avoid telling Ramesh about any of this.

12: When No One is Around

Tips that would have helped Chris

If a process is too time-consuming, or requires activities that seem to make no sense to them, people will find ways to work around it. SMEs are goaled on their technical work, not on their ability to fill out forms. Help them be successful and reduce their desire to go around the process. Build each process with their involvement, so it makes sense to them. Help them understand why it is important, and the purpose of everything they are asked to do.

A focus on tools and results comes naturally to most technical specialists. The process, or how they should work, does not. You should take every possible opportunity to educate them why it is important. Since SMEs can often get the support of other SMEs in achieving their objectives if process gets in the way, it is important for you to spread your educational message well beyond the teams directly involved in the areas you are currently improving.

CHAPTER 13: THE RIGHT THING THE WRONG WAY

"Who do you think you are?" snapped Brad, the data centre director, as he paced in front of Ramesh's desk, just as he had done since arriving 10 minutes ago. His face was red, like bad sunburn. Eyes wide, his speech was jerky and punctuated with sharp jabbing arm gestures. With greying hair looking a little like smoke, he acted like glowing coals about to flashover into a full blown firestorm.

He ignored me, and vented his anger on my manager, Ramesh, seemingly unwilling to waste the energy on me because of a confidence my chastisement would come at the hands of my own manager after he was done.

At my insistence, Ramesh had called in Chester, the change manager. Chester had worked for the company almost his entire career. Chester had built a huge network of friends across the company over the years, and could always be found at every after-hour's employee party buying drinks for the crowd. He only stumbled into the change manager role two years ago, when his old position was eliminated. His manager at the time had dropped him into that role to keep him from getting laid off.

Chester was not your typical change manager. Not only did he hate refusing change requests, he would go to almost any length to avoid it. He couldn't stand confrontation, and then dealing with the requestor's resulting frustration and objections. Fortunately, he was smart enough to assemble a change advisory board that complemented him well. They seemed to revel in confrontation and declining changes. That let him play the good cop, while they played the

13: The Right Thing the Wrong Way

heavy. Most of the time it worked ... except when changes in the process needed to be made. Then there was no one Chester could hide behind.

"Your team had no business interfering with the operations of my data centres," said Brad, poking his finger at Ramesh. "They don't belong in my data centre, and their presence there put critical business production operations in peril. Unlike some teams, we are essential to the day-to-day operations of the business. Without us, the company cannot conduct business. Without us, every person here would be out of a job."

Ramesh scowled. His eyes narrowed as he pursed his lips before speaking. Brad was organizationally his peer, in that they both reported to Jessica, but Brad was actually several levels higher from an HR perspective, and he treated Ramesh accordingly.

"Brad, will you just relax for a minute," said Ramesh. "Have a seat and let's talk about this civilly. We need to get beyond emotion and into facts."

"Facts! You want facts? Chris caused the damn outage! Now I've got to get on bended knee and beg Jessica's forgiveness, because I let someone into my data centre that shouldn't have been there. And I'll probably have to do the same for the CEO after that. If I don't get fired first."

Brad jerked a chair away from its place in front of Ramesh's desk and into the centre of the room. He didn't sit in it, but rather used it as a prop, slapping it and shaking it when making his point.

"Do you realize that Chris' stupidity took down key systems just as the new marketing program, Mountain Top, was about to be rolled out? Do you know how many

13: The Right Thing the Wrong Way

millions of dollars had been invested in this ... how many people had worked countless hours to make it happen? We're on a tight schedule to meet the requirements the business lays down."

Brad pointed a finger directly at Chester, who seemed to squirm under the attention. Brad was so upset, I could see his finger shaking from across the room. "Isn't that right, Chester? Just look at the volume of changes we get from change management. We can't slow down without impacting the rollout of all these new business programs."

"That's right," said Chester. "We have more change requests than ever."

Brad slapped the side of the chair and shook a finger straight at me. "And you screwed the whole thing up and nearly got yourself hurt in the process. It's a good thing you don't work for me, or you'd wish that rack had knocked your head in. And if I have my way, you'll be out of a job by this afternoon. We cannot afford to have bumbling meddlers like you in this company."

Ramesh glared at me and I knew that was the sign for me to sit quietly and just let Brad vent, but I wasn't going to let Brad's accusations stand. I hadn't done anything wrong. In fact, I'd done the right thing, and I wasn't going to let Brad intimidate me into being punished for doing the right thing.

I looked directly at Brad and calmly said, "I didn't cause the outage, Brad. There is plenty of blame to go around. It was a perfect storm of mistakes. Your team, the development team, and change management, each played a role in causing the incident. And the same chronic behaviors will continue to cause more outages unless

13: The Right Thing the Wrong Way

something is done about them, and the process used for making changes in the data centre."

For the first time since he'd walked in, Brad was totally silent. His eyes got wide and his mouth opened silently. He wasn't used to underlings pushing back on him when he was ranting. After an awkward moment, he mumbled incredulously, "What did you say?"

"I agree that I shouldn't have been able to get into the data centre last night. But then again, neither should the development team. And the fact that changes can be made without going through change management, only makes things worse. Your team, Brad, is the only team that should be in the data centre itself, and then, only when there is an approved change."

"It seems to me that you were the one we had to rescue from having a server rack nearly crush them on the floor," said Brad with a grin. "I think you would at least be a little grateful."

"I was in the data centre last night. Sure, that's right. But so were members of the development team. And the change management process isn't mature enough to ensure neither the development team, or I, was not there. Not to mention that your operations team should have thrown all of us out as soon as they spotted us. Cowboy installations that work outside the change management process should not be the accepted norm for your team."

"But that's not key here. It's not about pointing fingers," I said. "It's about figuring out how it happened, and preventing it from happening again. It's about root cause and remediation. It's about applying some problem management best practices."

13: The Right Thing the Wrong Way

Brad rolled his eyes and slowly shook his head, as he looked to the ceiling. "Please! Don't give me that ITIL crap again. I had to sit through more of your presentations on that than I cared to, and all of them were a waste of time."

"But Brad," added Ramesh. "Jessica has made a commitment to applying ITIL best practices where possible, to improve delivery of our services to the business. You've seen the data on how it helped cut back on our incidents. Remember … ?"

"Both of you have been swallowing too much of that consultant bull," snapped Brad. "I've been working in, and running data centres, for over 20 years. And I've done a damn good job at it. Hell, I've had this job for the last six years and outlived three CIOs so far. So I know I must be doing a good job, or they would have fired me by now."

"No one is questioning your experience, or your capabilities, Brad," said Ramesh, trying to defuse the emotion and get to the facts.

"They'd better not. Because I'll tell you, all this ITIL stuff is nothing new. I've taken the class. I know how it works. But guess what people, and you've probably not been around long enough to realize this. I've seen it all before … different names, different schemas … but never was there anything in there that any worthwhile data centre manager hasn't seen, or used before. ITIL just changed the name of everything, but there was nothing new in there that I didn't already know. I don't need it, and my data centres don't need it, no matter how much these consultants come in here and get leadership all in a panic. I run a tight ship, and the only time something goes wrong is when interlopers like Chris stumble around inside and muck things up."

13: The Right Thing the Wrong Way

Brad threw himself down in the chair. He seemed to have burned through some of his rage. His voice was calmer now. "What do I have to do to get some coffee around here? I always offer my guests coffee, no matter why they come to see me. It's not like you have to pay for it yourself, Ramesh."

Ramesh stepped outside for a moment and when he returned said, "Coffee is on its way."

Brad nodded and turned to me. "Why did you go into my data centre and start messing with environment? Are you malicious or just plain ignorant?"

"Because I saw people racking and stacking equipment in the production area."

Brad rolled his eyes. "You do realize that is what my people do, don't you? It's a data centre. We do adds, moves and changes in the facility. That's our job."

I shook my head. "These weren't your people. These were developers. They were doing this during a freeze period, and without approval from the change board."

I turned to Chester. "That's right, isn't it? They had no approved change request in the system."

Chester nodded slightly, and I could tell he was looking for a way to soft-pedal the situation. "Perhaps it was an emergency, and they were planning to complete the emergency change request documentation today, after the change. We have to assume positive intent. I'm sure they would never do anything to disrupt the company's objectives."

"No," I said. "It is okay to assume positive intent on the part of requestors, but that doesn't mean we can let them do

13: The Right Thing the Wrong Way

whatever they want ... and it doesn't mean we can let people make changes without going through the change management process. That's what the change advisory board is for. That's why we use leaders to be on that board; because they have a broader, and more integrated perspective, than the average technician. They are much better suited to know what will impact our business and what will not."

There was a knock at the door, and an administrative assistant wheeled in a cart with coffee on it. Brad took a cup, and placing it to his lips, took a huge gulp. "Jeez, Ramesh. You call that coffee? That's so weak, it makes green tea seem like a robust invigorating drink. If you want to know how to make real coffee, come down to my office and I'll show you how we make it the data centre way."

Before Ramesh could respond, the phone in the office rang. "This is Ramesh. Yes ... yes ... Brad and Chris and Chester. Okay, I'll put you on speakerphone."

Ramesh punched up the speakerphone. Jessica's voice came through loud and clear. And she was ticked.

"I just got done having several new orifices chewed into my body by both Jason and Sully, our CEO ... my boss. They've just educated me that, once again, IT broke something critical to the business, and did so at one of the worst possible times; that what should have been a simple change to the Mountain Top program, turned into a giant cluster. Not only didn't it get done, but somehow, we apparently broke some portions of the program that were working just fine."

Brad was the first to speak, "Jessica, this is Brad. It was because Chris ... "

13: The Right Thing the Wrong Way

Jessica cut him off. "Brad, I really don't care about the specifics. All of you are at the centre of this, and if you cannot work together to make this kind of problem go away, then I will have my admin order a silver platter to hold all the heads I'm going to deliver to the business. I don't want to see any fingers pointed among any of you. I don't care what you do, or how you do it, but this nonsense has to stop. Am I clear?"

Everyone in the room nodded silently. "Everyone here is aligned with you, Jessica," said Ramesh.

"Well I guess the message is clear," said Brad. "Don't do anything that may impact, or interfere, with the business needs. I know my team works that way, the question is; can the rest of the people here?"

I wasn't going to let Brad not change anything his team did. If they couldn't police their own space, there was no way we could prevent this type of issue going forward. "Will you at least tell your team to not let anyone into the data centre; much less do any work there. And that means anyone who is not part of your team?" I asked.

"So you want me to keep you out of the data centre? Is that it?" asked Brad with a grin, knowing that Jessica could not see him.

"Yes," I said. "And the development team, and the platform team, and any other team besides yours."

"Look, if I do that, then there is no way I can keep up with all of the requests coming through from the business," said Brad. "I just don't have the resources. The only way IT can keep meeting the business time lines is, if we use members of the development and platform teams to do some of the add/move/changes."

13: The Right Thing the Wrong Way

"But they are key contributors to the change related incidents. Aren't they Chester?"

"Well, there is only preliminary data," said Chester.

He was lying. I had worked with him over the last two weeks going through all of the change related incidents. The data was conclusive. Some of the teams were the source of a disproportionate number of change related incidents, and many of those involved business requests.

"But remember, Chester. How we were able to identify the teams involved in a high proportion of the incidents?"

"Yes, but I would like the chance to revisit the information. I don't want to point fingers at the wrong people. That would be very demotivating for our teams, and to tell the business that we can't meet their expectations for delivery would go against IT's basic charter as an organization."

"That's right, Chester," said Brad. "We all seem to easily forget that our whole reason for being here is to support the business, and meet their expectations when it comes to delivering new and current services. If we can't do that, then frankly they'd be better off outsourcing us."

"But we don't do them any favors if we simply agree to everything they ask for, even if we know it is not possible in a safe way," I said. "That may make them happy for the moment, but when we don't deliver, IT gets the reputation of being incompetent, unable to plan, and unable to deliver. The thing the business wants more than anything else is clarity and predictability. They may not like the answers we give them, but if we are honest and consistent, they may go back to trusting us as partners, instead of trying to out game us as suppliers, like they currently do. That honesty and transparency is what differentiates us from an outsourced

13: The Right Thing the Wrong Way

situation. If we can't partner with them in the true sense of the word, then we deserve to be outsourced, because they can't do any worse."

The room went silent for a moment. I hadn't really planned those words. They had just popped out. I felt good about them. They were perhaps not the most politic thing to say after Jessica's warning, but they needed to be said.

Jessica spoke first. "I think Chris has a point. Brad, I want you to lock down the data centre. Just so I am clear. You are responsible for whatever goes on there, whether your team does it or not. If there is a problem in the data centre, yours will be the first head on that platter. Do you understand?"

"Yes, ma'am," said Brad, as he began sending text messages to his team. "Consider it done. But in exchange, you've got to get change management to vet these things, not just for their doability, but also for our capability and capacity to make it happen on the schedule the business wants. Because I can tell you right now, we will be doing some serious pushback on the business requests." He paused, and took a long look at Chester. "As long as change management stands up to all the pressure and escalations from the business as well as the other IT teams, I'll execute only what they approve."

Jessica said, "Chester will need to step up and hold the line. That's his role and he needs to execute."

Chester looked like he wanted to disappear, until I said, "I'll back him up in the meetings, and with the information he needs to ensure we keep changes under control."

13: The Right Thing the Wrong Way

Ramesh looked at me and asked, "So you're taking accountability for managing the push-back on change requests? You and Chester are going to manage all of that?"

I nodded, half wondering what I had just impulsively gotten myself into. "If Chester wants the help, I'll partner with him."

Chester quickly nodded yes.

"Since I don't hear a 'no' from Chester, I'm assuming he's okay with it," said Jessica. "Okay Chris, I admire your initiative. Just remember that if anything gets through that should not, or people go around the process ... well, let's just say that I'll need sufficient room on that silver platter for two heads. Am I clear, Chris?"

I nodded, and sat their silent for a moment, until I remembered Jessica could not see me. "Yes," I said, as I wondered if I had gone too far this time.

13: The Right Thing the Wrong Way

Tips that would have helped Chris

The purpose of an ITSM project is not to replace what is in place. It is to improve IT's service to the user. First actions should include an assessment of what is in place, and determine what, if any, changes are necessary to improve the user experience. Too often ITSM initiatives are begun as slash and burn projects, where everything will be discarded, and a completely new, but only slightly different process, will replace it. That is wasteful, and encourages people to resist the changes. If it isn't broke, don't fix it.

Best practices are the accumulation of what has worked best for companies in a variety of situations. Not all aspects of best practice apply equally well for a given situation. You will find people who already perform some aspects of best practices, or close to them in their work. As long as it produces a good user experience, encourage them, even if they insist on using their own adaptation of it.

Producing small wins quickly will build credibility for your larger efforts, and make others more likely to invest their time and effort in your project. It will also encourage leadership to support you strongly. Try to deliver a noticeable success at least every 90 days, no matter how small the success. And don't forget to celebrate the win.

CHAPTER 14: GOING THROUGH THEM CHANGES

"Any questions?" I asked.

Ramesh sat speechless, staring at the slide projected on the wall of Jessica's office. The whir of the fan on the projector was the only sound. Jason had barely looked up during the entire presentation. He'd kept his nose buried in his tablet the whole time. Of course, Chester, the change manager, had dutifully followed along, but I didn't expect him to speak, unless asked a direct question. It just wasn't his style.

Jessica broke the silence. "Are you trying to tell me that 66% of all the incidents we have are due to activities approved by change management? The ones for the business, too?"

I nodded. "It's very consistent with what all the research and consulting organizations have found," I said. "If we never made any changes to our environment, we could reduce our service-impacting incidents to one-third their current level."

Jessica shook her head. "How can that be?"

"It's because our change management is designed to check the wrong things."

"I don't understand," said Jessica.

"Nearly 75% of the incidents we have now are due to errors by people, not failures of equipment or processes. Modern equipment is highly reliable, and with the more mature incident and problem management processes we put in,

14: Going Through them Changes

we've done the easy part, and gone about as far as we can without addressing the people part of the equation."

Ramesh interrupted me. "If you're telling us that the people in our IT organization are sub-standard. Why don't we just replace them?"

"No," I insisted.

I stood up in front of the whiteboard opposite the window. "Change management is all about deciding where the risks are, and how much of that risk we can tolerate. We can't change some risks, but many of them are under our control and can be reduced. Chester's right, there aren't enough hours or resources to put the same level of focus on everything. No change can ever get its risk to zero. We should be inspecting areas that present the most risk and where we can actually do things to reduce those risks."

I drew a big box labelled tools and technology risk. "Right now, change management assumes that the most likely source of incidents will be in the tools and technology. So that is what they focus on. It may have been true 20 years ago, but technology has changed. It's gotten more reliable and redundant. While there may still be some failures due to tools, it is definitely not the biggest risk." I redrew the box and made it much smaller.

I drew a large box next to it labelled, process risk. "Our change management assumes that the second most likely source of incidents is bad process; that there is some aspect of the review activity that we haven't taken into account. We've spent a lot of effort over the last few months tightening that up. So it's not the issue it used to be."

I redrew the process risk box much smaller, slightly bigger than the tools and technology box.

14: Going Through them Changes

"But our change management puts very little focus on the people element. Because so many of the issues are created by people, even small improvements in how people work to trap and prevent human errors, will leverage large reductions in the number of service disruptions."

"And how do you propose to go about doing that?" asked Jessica. "Are you looking to fire some people to get their attention and ensure they comply?" I could see by the look on Jessica's face that she was starting to connect the dots. It was beginning to make sense to her.

"Highly visible firings to put fear into the hearts of their peers, is about as effective as public executions. People will generally comply with what you want, only to the extent they avoid getting fired. Instead of digging into making the solutions better, they'll spend all their time covering their butts and looking for ways to deflect any blame to others. Compliance is what you get from bureaucratic threats. People will do the minimum as long as they can stand it, and the better ones will leave."

"Fear is a lousy motivator in IT. As leaders, we've got to create an environment, or process, that people are drawn to … something they embrace and want to make their own, because it meets their needs, and the needs of the company. Why do you think those developers ignored the change management process?"

"Because they were afraid their changes would not be approved. Too many changes are being denied?" asked Jessica.

I turned to Chester and asked, "What per cent of the change requests you get are denied, or delayed, by the change

14: Going Through them Changes

advisory board?" I knew the answer, but having him say it, gave the statistics that much more gravitas.

Chester flipped through some papers in a notebook and said, "Less than five per cent. But that's because we work really closely with the requestor before the meeting, to make sure everything that's needed is there, and any possible source of issue is resolved."

"I think I've seen data even lower than that, closer to two per cent," I added. "So fear of rejection is not very realistic."

"Okay," said Ramesh, "Spare us the drama. Why are people going around the change process?"

"People don't set out to do things they believe are bad. They just don't believe change management adds any value to what they do. They're confident in their abilities, and honestly believe they're doing the right thing for the company. They know what they are doing is right, and don't want to take the chance someone with less knowledge than they have, will deny an important business change."

Jason looked up from his tablet and said, "I definitely don't want that." I'd learned the hard way that although Jason may occasionally look like he is not engaged, he does seem to hear everything and forgets nothing … very useful skills in sales.

"Of course, Jason. None of us do," said Jessica, as she discretely wandered near Jason and tried to catch a glimpse of what he had been working on.

I found it funny how even people who had made it to the senior levels of leadership in the company, and now had legions of workers at their command, still retained that

14: Going Through them Changes

competitive drive and desire to one-up their peers. But habitual behavior is the hardest thing to change. They had used this behavior their entire careers, and that behavior was what led them to their current position, together with skill, and a decent amount of luck.

"We're like everyplace else. We've got an organization structure set up to tell people WHAT they should work towards. And as a first step, that's fine. People need to know what they should focus on to enhance the performance of the company. We even have a few of our better leaders who understand that the goal by itself is never enough. The way in which you get there is equally important. Without knowing the HOW we should achieve those goals, we might end up doing things in ways that are counter-productive to all of the other efforts going on. But the thing that almost all of our leaders fail to provide ... "

I paused for a moment and added, "And no offense, but this seems to be true at all levels. The thing that is always missing is the WHY. I'm not talking about some high-level lofty goals, although those are important. I'm talking about the rationale as to how this makes things better for everyone."

"Are you asking me and the other C-level leaders to justify their decisions to everyone in IT?" asked Jessica.

"No, it's not about justifying. It's about informing. If people understand the WHY, then they will know when things go awry that much sooner and respond. It helps people feel ownership of the activity."

"That's bullshit," said Jason, without even looking up from his tablet. "If I have to explain to my sales force why they

14: Going Through them Changes

should be closing deals, then they sure don't belong in sales."

"I agree," I said. "It's not telling them why closing deals is important. It's helping them understand why these prospects, these territories, these deals, get treated the way they do."

I drew a circle on the whiteboard. "Imagine this is my sphere of influence. It's the area where I am highly competent, and the area where most of my work occurs."

I drew a larger circle around the first circle. "This is my sphere of awareness. I may have some idea of what goes on in here, but it is not complete, and it is not necessarily accurate."

Then I drew another set of circles, but each much bigger in diameter than the first ones. "These are my leader's spheres of influence and awareness. Sometimes leaders forget that they have a much wider view of what's going on than their team does. So what to them seems like a commonly known rationale, is a corporate secret to those further down the organization, despite their needing it to do the best job possible."

"Leadership constantly deals with confidential information. Sometimes secrets have to remain that way for the good of the employees and the company," said Ramesh. "I can't tell you everything I know. For example, some of it would violate the privacy of other employees."

"You don't have to tell me everything. Just let me know why this particular WHAT you want done is more important than other similar WHATs. Tell me the benefits, not the specifics. It's good to keep confidential information private, just remember that in the absence of an

14: Going Through them Changes

explanation, people will always make up one of their own, and you are usually guaranteed that it will be much more unpleasant and negative than reality. We're dealing with people here, not machines."

Ramesh shook his head. "There is no way I'm going to start eating pink tofu and holding sessions with my team to start talking about our inner child."

Jessica looked confused. "So what's the big deal? If WHAT, HOW and WHY are the solution to this, why did you get us all together? Do you realize what the cost to the company is of having all of us together talking about something that I already told you to fix? You don't need my permission for every little thing you do."

"I wanted to show this to you for two reasons. First, to give you the good news that we should be able to show some real improvement very quickly if we can hold people accountable for quality of how they meet the goal, as well as the actual achievement of the goal; and second, to let you know in advance that not everyone is going to like this, especially if their changes get denied."

"I've sat in on some meetings," said Jessica. "I'm not one of those ivory tower CIOs you know. Not all changes get approved today. You just quoted us some figures. How is this any different?"

"The one type of change that causes a disproportionate impact is business changes. I'm talking about changes we make for the business at their request; whether updates to existing services' or rolling out business projects. Reducing incidents from those sources will leverage a big reduction in service disruptions."

14: Going Through them Changes

That caught Jason's attention. He set his tablet down and visibly paid attention.

"You're telling me that requests from the business are causing a lot of the disruptions in services to the business?" Jessica turned to Jason and asked, "Do you know this?"

"News to me," he said. "But I can't imagine we are the source of IT's service disruptions."

"You're not," I said. "Asking for a change doesn't cause an outage. It's the way IT designs the solution to your request, or implements the change. Maybe it's missing critical details, maybe the timing is bad, and maybe we had the wrong person doing it. It's not the businesses fault. It is still IT's fault."

"I'm glad to hear you say that. Now what are you going to do about it?" said Jason, as he went back to his tablet.

"You may not like the answer," I said. "It means we may have to delay, or halt, some of the business requests, until we are confident we've appropriately managed the risk of service disruptions. That means that you can't expect to turn in a request and expect us to implement it a couple of hours later."

Jason set the tablet down on the desk. "You don't understand. We have to react to conditions in the marketplace. Our customers don't give us the luxury of dawdling around until we're in the mood to make a critical change."

Jessica stepped in. "Absolutely, Jason. There are always urgent changes that need to be made quickly, whether because there is a service disruption, or because of a critical business issue. And we will always respond, and do

14: Going Through them Changes

everything we can in the time allotted to minimize risk. IT is here to support our business partners."

"That's true," I said. "But there are requests that are emergencies due to unforeseen situations requiting immediate remediation, and there are last minute changes due to poor planning on the part of the requestor."

I turned and gestured at Chester. "What did you find when you looked at the emergency changes; things that didn't get reviewed by the change advisory board until after the work had already been completed? What per cent of them were due to project roll-outs and other activities that should have been well planned in advance?"

Chester nervously shuffled through his notebook. He looked like a man who feared he would be fired at any moment. It was probably a realistic assessment, but at this point, I was tired of being the designated human sacrifice, and being thrown under the bus. If they wanted to fire me, so be it.

After a moment, Chester looked up and said, "Over 98% of the emergency change requests from the business were really just urgent changes due to poor planning on the requester's part. They were mostly things that the project manager, or business sponsor, or development team, knew were needed, but forgot to plan for."

"And those are just the ones we know about," I added. "There are probably dozens of other hardware and software changes cowboyed in completely outside the change management process. They are responsible for a huge number of our incidents." I paused for a moment to let the words sink in.

14: Going Through them Changes

"More importantly, not only is no one being held accountable for causing these service outages, but some people are actually getting rewarded despite them, because their portion of the project was completed on time. Effectively, they get rewarded for their piece of the project, even though the way they do it disrupts service to the business or the project itself. Through lack of oversight, we've given people the authority to use their own judgment as to whether or not they should follow the change management process, without holding them accountable for the result."

Ramesh shook his head and glared at Chester. "That sounds like failure, due to a poorly designed change management process, not a people failure."

"That may be the trigger, but the true root cause is that there are no consequences for inappropriate actions by people."

"Then I want to see some IT butts fired," said Jason as he turned to Jessica. "When people in sales fail, or seriously hurt the corporation like this, we get rid of them. I expect IT to be just as focused on the success of the company, and take the same type of action."

I spoke up before Jessica could react. "We should be careful how we do that," I said. "While individuals in IT, like the developers, or data centre crew, or change management team contribute to the incidents, the largest owner is leadership."

Jessica and Ramesh both scowled at me as I said, "And I am talking about all leadership, not just IT."

"Bullshit," said Jason. Visibly agitated, he was now standing and pointing at Jessica. "You can't blame the

14: Going Through them Changes

business for IT running amuck and breaking everything it touches."

Clearly, Jason was not accustomed to having underlings like I accuse his organization of contributing to their own problems. Jessica moved into damage control mode. "I don't think that is what Chris had in mind. Is it Chris?"

"What I am saying is that the business is a contributor to the frequency and impact of service disruptions, because they have a history of failing to give adequate notice for change requests, by not providing sufficient information about the change and ... " I looked over at Chester, who seemed to be trying to make himself as small and innocuous as possible in his chair. "By brow-beating anyone who attempts to ensure that above all else IT does no harm. Sure the IT team plays a part in it, but there is plenty of guilt to go around."

Jason was now addressing only Jessica. From his organizational perspective the rest of us had ceased to exist. "Jessica, if you think Sully is going to believe that sales is creating the problems ... "

"Incidents," I blurted out without realizing what I was doing. Jason stopped for an instant.

Ramesh leaned over and whispered, "Don't be any more of an idiot than you already are. Shut up and sit there or I promise you, I will fire you myself today."

"I really don't care if you call them cumquats, Jessica. Just know that I will not sit idly by while you deflect responsibility for your organization's failures," said Jason. "Remember I've been here for a number of years in this role. I've seen three other CIOs come and go. And all of them tried to do the same thing. My advice to you is to

14: Going Through them Changes

acknowledge your failures and come up with a remediation plan for tomorrow when we meet with Sully."

Jason snatched his things from the table and walked out of Jessica's office, slamming the door for effect.

Jessica turned to me and asked, "So what you're proposing as a way to further reduce incidents is to hold Brad accountable for ensuring no changes are made in our environment that haven't gone through some aspect of the change management process. You want me to make him the policeman?"

"It'll take more than Brad. He can only control the physicality in the data centre. Every one of your directs needs to hold their teams accountable for following change management processes, whether emergency, standard or normal changes. That includes development, support, engineering, and all the rest. There can be no more changes that go around the process because of a failure to plan on the part of some project manager, or anyone else. And you need the support of your peers in communicating the message to their teams that IT isn't doing this on a whim."

"The communication is your job, Chris, in case you forgot," said Jessica.

I nodded. "Okay, but they still need to understand that we're asking them to partner with us and work together to reduce service disruptions, because that benefits everyone. No one team owns it, nor can they make it happen. Everyone has to have some skin in the game, because if we don't work together, we will all fail separately."

She turned and walked over to me. Staring straight into my eyes, she asked, "And you are absolutely positive that this

14: Going Through them Changes

will quickly provide a dramatic reduction in the number of service impacting incidents?"

I nodded. "We need to make a few tweaks to the change advisory board to refocus their review more on the people side, and less on the technology side. And we need to make being on the CAB less of an honorary, to be added to your resume and requires no heavy lifting. The members of the CAB need to be held accountable for failed changes that should have been caught during their review. But we can handle that as part of problem management."

Jessica nodded, "And of course to refuse business change requests."

"Not the way I'd put it. We're not going to prevent the change, just do a better job of making sure everything is in order to reduce the chance of disruptions before we begin. So it's not really a refusal, just a rescheduling."

Jessica ran her finger around the edge of the window and murmured, "I did so like having this office."

She turned and walked over to me. Staring straight into my eyes, she asked me again, as if trying to convince herself, "And you are absolutely positive that this will quickly provide a dramatic reduction in the number of service impacting incidents?"

I nodded.

"Well, I can take the heat for a little while, as long as we deliver on the reductions," said Jessica.

"I'd stake my life on it," I said.

Jessica smiled at me and replied, "No need to go quite that far yet, Chris, but you are definitely staking your job on it."

14: Going Through them Changes

> **Tips that would have helped Chris**
>
> The source of most IT incidents can be traced to the actions of people. Often this is due to a mistake. However, sometimes it is due to the person not understanding "Why" something is important, and making a bad decision when faced with changing circumstances. No set of instructions can cover all possible turns of events. That is why people are often used to cover critical tasks. Most of the time we give people the "What" we need done. We usually give them the "How" we want it done in procedures and instructions. What we often fail to give them is the "Why". Knowing the "Why" allows them to adapt to unforeseen situations, even if that adaptation is realizing the "What" cannot continue and they should call for help. Always give people the "What", "How" and "Why".
>
> When trying to reduce the number of human errors, it is easy to penalize the person responsible for the mistake, and hold them up as an example of what not to do. Everyone will make mistakes. Focusing on them with an expectation that IT will be 100% perfect is unrealistic. A better course is to focus on, and reward those people and teams who are making fewer mistakes. It encourages a sense of accountability and ownership, not to mention increasing morale and reducing the number of mistakes.

CHAPTER 15: SOME FINGERS POINT AND SOME HANDS CLAP

The change management meeting had gone well, right up to the point where the fourth of six business change requests had been denied. Meredith played her part as the aggrieved party quite well, despite the fact that the business had tried to push them out into production as emergency changes two days earlier. The rationale for the emergency was the potential loss of revenue if the latest fix to Mountain Top was not enabled in time. But the reality had been that they hadn't even considered working through the change management process until Brad's team refused to cooperate.

The developers had apparently been told by their leader, that if any of them went outside the change management process, regardless of who asked them, they would be summarily fired and walked out the door that day. I had also been told that Brad had given his teams a similar message, although with a much more colorful and scatological description of the hurt that he would rain down on them if they even thought about ignoring change management process.

It seemed Jessica had been true to her word, and made it very clear to her directs that as long as she was CIO, the penalty for deviating from the established change management process would be terminal. And with the constant reinforcing support from the change advisory board members, even Chester seemed to have grown a tiny bit less apprehensive about declining change requests.

15: Some Fingers Point and Some Hands Clap

Things did seem to be falling into place, and based on the preliminary data I was seeing, our incidents due to changes were declining. With continued hard work and co-operation, not to mention a tiny bit of luck, we'd be able to give Jessica that noticeable decline in change related incidents.

But when that fourth change request was denied at the meeting, all it took was a single message from Meredith to Jason to have us all standing outside the office of Sully, the CEO, a few hours later. It had originally been set-up as just Jessica, Jason and Sully. But Jessica had insisted I be there. Ramesh, with his well-hewn corporate survival instincts, found he had a family medical crisis and was able to wriggle out. Jason was there of course, as was Meredith.

I found it ironic that the four of us were standing outside Sully's office. We knew each other well and worked together on a day-to-day basis. We chatted about upcoming items we needed to co-operate on. Jason even shared most of the few jokes he knew that could be told in an office environment. But no one mentioned, or even hinted, at the issue that had brought us here. I just couldn't do it. After this, I wasn't sure I could go back to working with Meredith or Jason again. They were doing the wrong thing for the company and the employees, and I was not about to be their friend.

As I sat there watching them mingle, I remembered a time when I watched attorneys outside a courtroom prior to a trial. They were friendly, making plans for lunch the next day, and sharing information about upcoming cases. But once in the courtroom they became total competitors, doing anything within the bounds of legal protocol to win for their

15: Some Fingers Point and Some Hands Clap

client. Afterwards, I saw them outside just as friendly as they had been before the trial.

At first I thought they had simply compartmentalized their lives, but when I overheard them giving each other notes and compliments on the way they advocated for their clients during the trial, I realized it was more than that. They had, either through training or through inclination, learned how to be fact-based in their working relationship. When the facts of their individual roles required them to be adversaries, they were. When the facts of their individual roles allowed them to be allies, they were. But in the long run, they were willing to set aside their differences and work together for the good of the entire process.

I realized that was how I needed to be. No matter what the issue, it was about the facts. People's roles change. Circumstances change. And sometimes we are bound to be in conflict. But that doesn't change the underlying relationships we all build. I could not be successful in IT, or anywhere else in business, if I took situational opposition personally. And those people that did, would eventually become isolated, trusting only themselves and no one else.

I supposed that made me open to suffering at the hands of people who made everything personal and could never get beyond. But I also knew that no one of us can ever be as strong as all of us.

Exactly 20 minutes late, the door to Sully's office opened and three people, whose photographs I recognized from the annual report, walked out. They were senior members of the board; old men wearing very expensive suits and walking with that calm measured pace of those who were used to others getting out of their way. Each had been a highly successful executive, or investor, in their day. Now

15: Some Fingers Point and Some Hands Clap

they spent their retirement advising others on how to best operate. Their conversation was full of light banter, back slapping and polite laughter. It was not about the company or business issues. It was all about promises to get together after the next board meeting to spend the day sailing on another board member's boat. Everyone was all smiles and firm handshakes. I wondered if the same conversation inside had been just as genial.

None of them acknowledged us as we stood silently and watched Sully walk them down the hall toward the elevator. He returned a few minutes later. He held up his hand to us and quietly said, "Give me a moment, please," before stepping into his office and closing the door behind him.

The phone lines on his assistant's desk lit up, indicating he was making some calls. After about 15 minutes, he opened the door, face still full of smiles, and motioned for us all to come in. "Sorry for the delay."

Sully's office was large by company standards, but more importantly, he had a private conference room adjacent to it. That room had seats for 10. Sully stood between us and his desk, and gestured for us to proceed directly into his conference room.

After waiting for everyone to find their place and sit down, Sully took his place at the head of the table. His tone immediately changed.

"Why have you taken this time from me?" he asked with a scowl. "Why are you making me spend my time with you now, instead of letting me run the company?"

"You called this meeting," said Jessica. "You wanted to talk about change management."

15: Some Fingers Point and Some Hands Clap

"Technically correct," said Sully. "But the reason I called the meeting is that like a bunch of children in the schoolyard, you can't learn how to play together. But unlike the schoolyard, because you are incapable of working together, it negatively impacts the company, its customers and its stockholders."

"Look," he said in a loud directive voice that filled the room. "I hear what's going on. People talk to me. I ask questions. This is not my first day on the job. We give funding to you for your IT team, with the expectation that it is going to be used to deliver projects the business needs ... delivered on-time, on-budget and with the functionality they need. And all I've been getting lately are complaints ... distractions I don't need when I'm practically killing myself trying to get the Board of Directors to make some additional investments in the company."

"Sully, my team does a lot of work to sustain the business ... work that isn't on your project list and is important to keeping the lights on and the business working."

"Jessica, you are not hearing me. Every one of your CIO predecessors has used that same song and dance to justify why their organization has less financial discipline than an eight year old child does. Note that I say predecessors, those former CIOs who were unleashed to achieve even higher levels of success elsewhere. Fixing this comes with the territory of being CIO. It's why you get paid the big bucks."

"And you, Jason," said Sully. "I hear your team likes to do it all."

"We're proud of the company, Sully, and we'll do anything necessary to make it a success," said Jason.

15: Some Fingers Point and Some Hands Clap

"Well then stop messing around in the IT space. Unless I'm mistaken, I pay you to sell products and services. You're here to close deals that bring in revenue, not rack and stack hardware."

"But if we don't do it, IT will never meet our deadline. They have everything bottled up with their change management bureaucrats."

"Sorry, that won't fly," said Sully. "I've seen the data. Given how many of the incidents are self-inflicted by your team's actions and requests, I think they may not be tough enough. Instead of skulking around the data centre, spend some of that time doing a better job of planning your new programs. Hold IT accountable for delivering what you need on time, and in good working order, but always remember this. A failure to plan on your part does not constitute an emergency on their part."

Sully waved his finger at Jason. "If I hear any more about you thinking that you're the VP of sales, marketing and IT, then I may set you free and start talking to all those eager-eyed and hungry sales executives the board keeps referring to me. Am I clear?"

Jason nodded and mumbled, "Yes sir."

"Look, your teams have made some great progress so far in reducing incidents and problems. You've got to keep working together to make it even better."

Sully paused and looked around the room. "Any questions?"

No one spoke.

15: Some Fingers Point and Some Hands Clap

"Good," said Sully as he picked up the receiver on his phone. "Now get out of here. I have to go move some mountains. This meeting is over. Good-bye."

I was the last leaving Sully's office, and as I closed his door I mumbled something, wondering how he knew so much about what had been going on with all the work we had done and the data we had found.

Sully's administrative assistant, Tomisha, sat right outside his door. She'd worked for Sully for many years, and she always seemed to have a smile for me.

I'd followed Meredith's advice and made sure I sent birthday cards to all of the administrative assistants in IT and corporate. And Tomisha's had gone out about a month ago. I doubt that was why she was pleasant with me. She was probably just a nice person.

As I passed her desk, Tomisha stopped what she was doing, smiled and whispered, "Chester plays 18 holes of golf with Sully every weekend. Chester is a scratch golfer and Sully has a 10 handicap, but Chester always lets Sully win."

I was smiling as I walked away and made a mental note to do something nice for Meredith; and Chester, too.

15: Some Fingers Point and Some Hands Clap

Tips that would have helped Chris

Try to keep your users out of the business of operating IT. When users get involved in the mechanics of how the components in services are assembled, or the way in which they are supplied, it usually means IT has failed to deliver the kinds of services users need. Out of frustration, users step in to do the work for you. IT is not their strength, so you spend much of your time explaining component details to them. It's not what they are paid for. Time they spend trying to be IT, means less time doing the work they need to do to keep the business running. And that hurts everyone. This behavior is not their fault. IT is at fault for not delivering what their customers need. When you start an ITSM project and encounter this, be forewarned that you will need to also address the issue of increasing their trust and comfort level that IT will deliver. To gain their trust, you will need to give them your trust. Treat them like a partner, but always remember they are a partner you serve. Without them, there is no reason for your position in the company.

CHAPTER 16: WHAT HAVE YOU DONE FOR ME TODAY?

Sully's resonant baritone voice filled the room from the speakerphone. "Jessica, all I want is a simple answer to a simple question. Will you meet the delivery timeline Mountain Top phase II?"

Jessica shook her head silently, and then said, "Sorry Sully. No, we can't. There just aren't enough resources in IT to get it done."

Sully cut her off and finished her sentence. "Jessica, stop. No excuses or explanations. We're talking about almost 120 days from now. And you're telling me you can't divert enough resources to meet this critical business need? This can't go on. I want the business projects delivered first, and then your team can go off and play with their shiny toys. Do you understand me?"

From the look on Jessica's face, I knew she wanted to take the call private, but there was no handset on the speakerphone and it was the only conference room. "Sully, my team does a lot of work to sustain the business ... work that isn't on your project list, and is important to keeping the business working. Can you wait a moment so I can deal with something here?"

She waved at us and pointed to the door. Quickly we headed out. The last thing I heard, as I closed the door behind us, was Sully's booming voice.

"Jessica, you are not hearing me. Every one of your CIO predecessors used that same song and dance to justify why their organization has less financial discipline than an eight

16: What Have you Done for me Today?

year old child. Note that I say predecessors ... former CIOs who were unleashed to achieve even higher levels of success elsewhere. Fixing this comes with the territory of being CIO. It's why you get paid the big bucks. So fix it. I expect an update on your progress at our one-on-one next week."

I don't think Jessica expected to get chastised by her manager on this call. If she had, she definitely wouldn't have allowed us to be there. It had been uncomfortable to listen in to even that little bit of their conversation. I guess it doesn't really matter what your level is. We all get chewed out by our boss at some point.

I walked over to Meredith's cube and sat down across the desk from her.

"I understand the business is not happy with the way we're delivering projects," I said.

"Actually, no. IT is very good at delivering projects on time, on budget, and on specification ... their own projects that is. Ours get ignored unless someone in IT is bored and has nothing else to do. And frankly, that's backwards."

"That's not true," I countered.

We spent the next 10 minutes citing anecdotal examples of how IT had, or had not, delivered what was expected and delivered it on time. There was going to be no traction. Neither group was going to give up its perception of what was happening. Unfortunately, the business, as always, had a much bigger voice to complain with, because if they weren't around, there would be no need for IT to be around. They brought in all the money. All we did was spend it.

16: What Have you Done for me Today?

Finally, I said, "We could go on like this all day. There must be some rational way resources are allocated, right?"

Meredith laughed. "You are even more naive than I thought. Follow me. It will open your eyes."

Meredith took me to a conference room packed with an even mix of leaders from IT and the business. Ramesh and Jessica were there, as were Jason and a number of his direct reports.

Jason spoke first. "Okay, listen up. This is a new project we need delivered within 180 days. It's called Rubber Boots, and is an enhancement to the inventory management system that will allow the stores to get real-time information on product availability, as well as replenishment times. It's been through your technical teams, so the specifics should be pretty clear."

"I haven't seen it," said Hiu. "And I don't know if it will work without some network modifications."

"Me neither," said Clement. "How much space do you need in the data centre? Do you have speeds and feeds requirements for me?"

"You were supposed to pick it up from my admin," said Ramesh. "I sent you a note about it last week."

"That explains it," said Clement. "I never read any of your e-mails, Ramesh."

Everyone laughed until Jason said, "Cut the crap. Give me a show of hands as to how many have reviewed this proposal."

Less than half the IT hands went up.

16: What Have you Done for me Today?

"Are you kidding me?" yelled Jason. "Do any of you techies actually care whether we make any money or not? Are there any adults working in IT?"

From somewhere in the crowd came a muffled, half giggling, "No."

"Stop that. This is serious business," said Jessica. "I'm sorry but it's moot, Jason. IT resources are fully allocated for the next year. Even if they had read it, there is nothing we can do to make it happen. You will just have to replan it for a year from now."

"A year from now it will be obsolescent at best. Can't IT do anything? Isn't anyone in IT in charge of planning programs and projects?"

"If you recall," offered Ramesh. "We did request heads for a program and project planning team during the budget cycle, but it ended up being rejected in favour of opening some new sales offices."

"At least they bring in revenue," said Meredith.

"So what if your request got rejected," insisted Jason. "Do what we do in sales and marketing. Adapt, improvise, overcome. We do what it takes to work around obstacles. Why don't you just reassign someone from your existing team to put the process together? Think of all the time you would save and the additional money the company could generate."

With a sarcastic, nearly rhetorical, tone, Jessica asked, "Oh and did you have someone specific in mind, Jason? Someone in IT you trust enough to make this work?"

Jason stood mute for a moment, and then scanned the room.

16: What Have you Done for me Today?

"Yes I do. I have someone in mind. I'll even carve enough money out of my project budget to fund it, if that person is put in charge."

Jason stuck out his arm and pointed directly at me.

"Chris."

"Chris?" questioned Ramesh.

"Yes, Chris," said Jason. After the progress we made on reducing the incidents, this is just the kind of challenge Chris should be eager for. We want Chris for the role."

Jessica never even looked at me. She just nodded and said, "Chris it is."

16: What Have you Done for me Today?

Tips that would have helped Chris

ITSM is built on repeating cycles, like the Deming Cycle, the ITIL life cycle, and the whole concept of continual improvement. When you are successful in implementing elements of an ITSM process, you will be first choice for the next confusing, or complicated, process issue. The price of success is dealing with even more challenging issues as the cycle of learning begins again.

If you were Chris, would you take on this new assignment, even though it will require solving service and demand portfolio management, service catalogue, service desk and request fulfilment issues? I think you would.

The question is, can Chris make it happen in the next book and not get fired in the process?

ITG RESOURCES

IT Governance Ltd sources, creates and delivers products and services to meet the real-world, evolving IT governance needs of today's organizations, directors, managers and practitioners.

The ITG website (*www.itgovernance.co.uk*) is the international one-stop-shop for corporate and IT governance information, advice, guidance, books, tools, training and consultancy.

www.itgovernance.co.uk/itsm.aspx is the information page on our website for ITSM resources.

Other Websites

Books and tools published by IT Governance Publishing (ITGP) are available from all business booksellers and are also immediately available from the following websites:

www.itgovernance.co.uk/catalog/355 provides information and online purchasing facilities for every currently available book published by ITGP.

www.itgovernance.eu is our euro-denominated website which ships from Benelux and has a growing range of books in European languages other than English.

www.itgovernanceusa.com is a US$-based website that delivers the full range of IT Governance products to North America, and ships from within the continental US.

www.itgovernanceasia.com provides a selected range of ITGP products specifically for customers in South Asia.

www.27001.com is the IT Governance Ltd website that deals specifically with information security management, and ships from within the continental US.

ITG Resources

Pocket Guides

For full details of the entire range of pocket guides, simply follow the links at *www.itgovernance.co.uk/publishing.aspx*.

Toolkits

ITG's unique range of toolkits includes the IT Governance Framework Toolkit, which contains all the tools and guidance that you will need in order to develop and implement an appropriate IT governance framework for your organization. Full details can be found at *www.itgovernance.co.uk/products/519*.

For a free paper on how to use the proprietary Calder-Moir IT Governance Framework, and for a free trial version of the toolkit, see *www.itgovernance.co.uk/calder_moir.aspx*.

There is also a wide range of toolkits to simplify implementation of management systems, such as an ISO/IEC 27001 ISMS or a BS25999 BCMS, and these can all be viewed and purchased online at: *www.itgovernance.co.uk/catalog/1*.

Best Practice Reports

ITG's range of Best Practice Reports is now at *www.itgovernance.co.uk/best-practice-reports.aspx*. These offer you essential, pertinent, expertly researched information, on a number of key issues, including Web 2.0 and Green IT.

Training and Consultancy

IT Governance also offers training and consultancy services across the entire spectrum of disciplines in the information governance arena. Details of training courses can be accessed at *www.itgovernance.co.uk/training.aspx* and descriptions of

ITG Resources

our consultancy services can be found at *www.itgovernance.co.uk/consulting.aspx*. Why not contact us to see how we could help you and your organization?

Newsletter

IT governance is one of the hottest topics in business today, not least because it is also the fastest moving, so what better way to keep up than by subscribing to ITG's free monthly newsletter Sentinel? It provides monthly updates and resources across the whole spectrum of IT governance subject matter, including risk management, information security, ITIL and IT service management, project governance, compliance and so much more. Subscribe for your free copy at: *www.itgovernance.co.uk/newsletter.aspx*.